Frantic Assembly presents

# RABBIT

## by Brendan Cowell

first performance of this production Friday 12 September 2003

# Rabbit

## Autumn Tour Schedule 2003

| | |
|---|---|
| **12 – 27 September** | Drum Theatre, Plymouth |
| **30 September & 1 October** | South Hill Park, Bracknell |
| **2 – 4 October** | Trinity Theatre, Tunbridge Wells |
| **7 & 8 October** | Gardner Arts Centre, Brighton |
| **10 & 11 October** | Northern Stage, Newcastle Playhouse |
| **13 & 14 October** | The Point, Eastleigh |
| **15 & 16 October** | Stantonbury Theatre, Milton Keynes |
| **20 – 25 October** | Lyric Hammersmith, London |
| **28 & 29 October** | Arena Theatre, Wolverhampton |
| **30 October** | Alsager Arts Centre, Alsager |
| **4 & 5 November** | Phoenix Arts, Leicester |
| **6 – 8 November** | Lakeside Arts Centre, Nottingham |
| **12 – 15 November** | Contact Theatre, Manchester |
| **17 & 18 November** | Lawrence Batley Theatre, Huddersfield |
| **19 November** | The Hawth Theatre, Crawley |
| **20 – 22 November** | Pegasus Theatre, Oxford |
| **24 & 25 November** | Norwich Playhouse, Norwich |
| **26 – 28 November** | Warwick Arts Centre, Coventry |

# Cast

| | |
|---|---|
| Sam Crane | **Spin** |
| Helen Heaslip | **Madeline Cave** |
| Susan Kyd | **Kate Cave** |
| David Sibley | **Paul Cave** |
| Karl Sullivan | **The Driver** |
| | |
| Written by | Brendan Cowell |
| Directors | Scott Graham |
| | Steven Hoggett |
| Choreographed by | Scott Graham |
| | Steven Hoggett |
| | Karl Sullivan |
| Design | Dick Bird |
| Lighting Design | Giuseppe di Iorio |
| Featuring music | Deadly Avenger |
| Additional music | Thomas Newman |
| | Carter Burnwell |
| Production Manager | Jai Lusser |
| Company Stage Manager | Tom Cotterill |
| Technical Stage Manager | Heidi Riley |
| Set Build | Adrian Snell |
| Props Maker | Paula Eden |
| Sound Effects | Nick Manning |
| Sound Track | Steven Hoggett |
| Costume Supervisor | Hattie Barsby |
| Production Runner | Hannah Powell |
| Producer | Vicki Middleton |
| Administrator | Sinead MacManus |
| PR / Company Associate | Ben Chamberlain, |
| | Chamberlain McAuley |
| Graphic Design | Emma Cooke |
| | Chamberlain McAuley |
| Marketing Manager | Clair Chamberlain |
| | Chamberlain McAuley |

**Thanks to:**
Susie Lindemann for kicking it all off (keep it off!), Will Sheehan at Griffin Theatre, Sydney for such sweet generosity, Michael Wynne and John Cannon for being a light when casting got dark, Kim Brandstrup, John Tiffany and Vicky Featherstone for knowing us better than we know ourselves, Simon Mellor, Marco Favaro – da best, the newly weds Nick Middleton and Sian Graham, Simon Stokes and all the lovely people at TRP, Cecilia Ritchie, John Isaacs, New Empire Theatre, Southend-on-Sea, The Settle Inn, Battersea, Steve Wald and Perou.

# Biographies

### Sam Crane – Spin

After studying classics at Oxford University, Sam trained at LAMDA. His theatre credits include Berenger in *Rhinoceros* (Oxford Playhouse), Tadeusz Kantor and Soldier in *A Little Requiem for Kantor* (London International Mime Festival and SESC Theatre, Sao Paulo), Autolycus in *The Winter's Tale* (Ouds Japan Tour), Fool in *King Lear* and the title role in *Hamlet* (The Old Fire Station, Oxford), *Boyband*, *Square Root of Minus One* and *Red Magic* (Edinburgh Festival) and Alan in *Equus* (Burton Taylor Theatre). TV work includes Daniel Talbot in *Midsomer Murders* (ITV) and Jason in *The Sins* (BBC). Sam has performed numerous radio plays for BBC Radio Drama.

### Helen Heaslip – Madeline Cave

Helen trained at Arts Educational. She is a member of The Impulse Company. Theatre credits include *10 Short Plays* (Paines Plough), Mairead – understudy and played – in *The Lieutenant of Inishmore* (The Garrick), Runt in *Disco Pigs* (Goldsmiths Theatre), Rochamabodi in *Slipping Consonants* (Tour), Laura in *Through the Shadows* (Tour), Fran in *Whale Music*, Eliza Doolittle in *Pygmalion* (Richmond), Jane in *Crystal Clear* (Formby Studio), Ratty in *Toad of Toad Hall* (Open Air Theatre). TV credits include *Wild Horses*, *The Things They Do for Love*, *Emmerdale*, *Lyddie*. Film credits include *Partisan*, *Interruption*, *Queen's Park*, *O.U.T.*

### Susan Kyd – Kate Cave

Trained at LAMDA, Ecole Jacques Lecoq and Central St Martin's School of Art. Theatre includes premiere of Steven Berkoff's *West* (Donmar Warehouse), *Pal Joey!* (Half Moon and Albery), *Time and the Conways* (Old Vic and Royal Alexandra Toronto). Repertory *What the Butler Saw*, *Les Liaisons Dangereuses*, *Servant of Two Masters*, *An Ideal Husband*, *Hay Fever*, *Noises Off*, *A Family Affair*, *The Real Thing*, *The Master Builder*, *Blithe Spirit*, *The Provok'd Wife*, *A Midsummer Night's Dream* and *The Importance of Being Earnest*. Television includes *Inspector Morse*, *Casualty*, *Victoria and Albert*, *Married for Life*, *Up the Garden Path*, *Lovejoy*, *Minder*, *Bugs*, *Allo Allo*, *Coronation Street*, *Spacevets*, *Animal Ark*, *Dream Team*, *The Bill* and *West*. Radio includes *Dandy Dick*, *A Tough Business*. Film includes *A Business Affair* and *Dance With a Stranger*.

### David Sibley – Paul Cave

David trained at Drama Centre. Theatre credits include *Midsummer Night's Dream* (Bristol Old Vic), *Pistols* (The Drum Theatre), *King Lear* (Almeida), *Beckett's Words and Music* (Birmingham Contemporary Music Group), *Some Explicit Polaroids* (Out of Joint and West End), *Naked* (Almeida and West End), *Positive Hour* (Out of Joint and Hampstead), *Lion in the*

*Streets* (Hampstead), *Belonging* (Cheltenham Festival), *The Great Highway* (Gate), *Turning Over* (Bush), *Hamlet* (Royal Court). TV credits include *Love Again, A&E, Attachments, Judge John Deed, Care, Drovers Gold, Frontiers, The Big One, Middlemarch, Redemption, Young Indy, The Nightmare Years, Wilderness Road, The Manageress, Stars of the Roller State Disco, The Kitchen* and *The Fatal Spring*. Film credits include *Incognito, Princess Cariboo, Ghandi, Willow.*

## Karl Sullivan – Driver

Karl studied business and mathematics at the University of Hertfordshire before training at the Northern School of Contemporary Dance. He went on to train at the Rambert Dance School during which time he performed with Moving Visions Dance Theatre and National Youth Dance Company. Frantic credits include *Hymns*. Karl has also worked with Arc Dance Company, V-TOL, Matthew Hawkins, Deborah Johnson, Union Dance Company, Diversions Dance Company and Adventures in Motion Pictures *Swan Lake*. In Ireland, Karl has worked with Irish Modern Dance Theatre, Cois Ceim Dance Theatre and Dance Theatre of Ireland.

## Brendan Cowell – Writer

Twenty-seven year old Brendan is one of Australia's most exciting young writers. This year he received the prestigious Griffin Award for new Australian work for *Rabbit*, which premiered at Sydney's Griffin Theatre in April under the direction of Kate Gaul. His previous plays include *Men* (Old Fitzroy, downstairs Belvoir St), *Happy New* (Old Fitzroy), *ATM* (2002 Sydney Festival) and *Bed,* for which he was awarded the 2001 Patrick White Playwrights' Award. In the same year, Brendan was awarded a Gloria Payten / Gloria Dawn Foundation Young Artist Award, which took the form of a travel grant that allowed him to visit the UK and Europe. Brendan is about to complete a new play *Morph*, which was commissioned by the Sydney Theatre Company's Blueprints Literary Program and will premiere in November with Benjamin Winspear directing. Brendan has feature projects in development with Mushroom Pictures and Icon Shanahan Productions.

## Steven Hoggett – Director

Steven is co-founder and Artistic Director with Frantic Assembly. Director / performer credits for Frantic include *Look Back in Anger, Klub, Flesh, Zero, Sell Out, Hymns, Heavenly* and *Tiny Dynamite* (co-production with Paines Plough). Directorial credits include *Underworld* and *Peepshow* for Frantic, *Service Charge* (Lyric Theatre, Hammersmith) and *Air* (MAC, Birmingham). Co-direction and choreography credits include *Vs.* (with Karim Tonsi Dance Company, Cairo), *Waving* (Oily Carte), *Improper* (Bare Bones Dance Company), *Subterrain* (Farm Productions) and *The Straits* (Paines Plough). Additional performance credits include *Manifesto* (Volcano Theatre Company), *Go Las Vegas* (The Featherstonehaughs) and *Outside Now* for Prada (Milan Fashion week 2001).

## Scott Graham – Director

Scott is co-founder and Artistic Director with Frantic Assembly. Director / performer credits for Frantic include *Look Back in Anger, Klub, Flesh, Zero, Sell Out, Hymns, Heavenly* and *Tiny Dynamite* (co-production with Paines Plough). Directorial credits include *Underworld* and *Peepshow* for Frantic, *Service Charge* (Lyric Theatre, Hammersmith) and *Air* (MAC, Birmingham). Co-direction and choreography credits include *Vs.* (with Karim Tonsi Dance Company, Cairo), *Subterrain* (Farm Productions) and *Improper* (Bare Bones Dance Company). Additional performance credits include *Outside Now* for Prada (Milan Fashion week 2001).

## Dick Bird – Designer

Dick Bird's recent designs *Thwaite* (Almedia Opera), *Messalina* (The Battignano Opera Festival), *The Lucky Ones* (Hampstead Theatre), *Misconceptions* (Derby and Salisbury Playhouse), *Great Expectations* (Bristol Old Vic), *Ben Hur* (BAC), *Mr Placebo* (Traverse Theatre), *Flesh Wound* (Royal Court), *The Banquet* (Protein Dance), *Monkey!* (Young Vic), *A Prayer for Owen Meany* and *The Walls* (Royal National Theatre), *The Lady in the Van* (West Yorkshire Playhouse), *My Fair Lady* and *Closer* (Teatro El Nacional, Buenos Aires), *Il Tabarro* and *Vollo di Notte* (Long Beach Opera in California), *Light* (Theatre de Complicite) and *The Three Musketeers* (Young Vic). He has worked extensively with Primitive Science including *Vagabondage, Icarus Falling, Poseidon* and most recently *The Invisible College* at the Salzburg Festival. Previously for Frantic Assembly, *Peepshow* and *Heavenly*.

## Giuseppe di Iorio – Lighting Design

Current and recent lighting design includes *Faust* (National Opera of Rome and Turin Opera), *King Priam* and *Turn of the Screw* (Nationale Reisopera Holland), *Elsa Canasta* (Rambert Dance Company), *Simon Boccanegra* (Teatro Verdi, Trieste), *The Damnation of Faust* (Opera North), *Little Magic Flute* (Opera North Education), *Fidelio* and *Tosca* (Holland Park Opera), *Aida* (Teatro Lirico Cagliari), *Romanza una Favola* (Rome Opera), *The Banquet* (Goldoni Theatre, Florence), *Macbeth* (set and lighting, Munster), *Tall Stories* (The Shout, Vienna), *La Traviata* (Malmo, Sweden), *Il Giuramento, Mirandolina* and *Manon Lescaut* (Wexford), *L'Etoile* (Guildhall), *Young Man with Carnation* (Almeida Opera and Buxton), *Tom's Midnight Garden* (Contact Theatre, Manchester), *The Possessed* (Athens Opera), *Der Zwerg* (Turin), *Going to Shadows* (Guildhall School and Brisbane Academy) and *Xerxes* (National Opera of Greece).

Featuring music by **Deadly Avenger.** Written, arranged and performed by Deadly Avenger. Taken from the album, *Deep Red*, available on Illicit Recordings, ILLCD002. www.deadlyavenger.com. www.illicitrecordings.com

## Jai Lusser – Production Manager

Previous Production Manager credits include *Peepshow, Heavenly* (Frantic Assembly), *Stomp* (European and Far East Tour), *A House of Correction* (The Wrestling School), *The Magic Flute* (Garden Opera), *Maps of Desire* (Wonderful Beast) and *BOING!* (Oily Cart). He has also worked as Production Manager for The Pleasance in Edinburgh as part of a working relationship spanning five years. Jai has worked regularly with The Wrestling School including the eight-hour *The Ecstatic Bible* (Adelaide Festival) and English Touring Theatre including *The York Realist* (Royal Court and West End). Other credits include *Baddiel and Skinner Unplanned, Lulu* (Almeida, King's Cross), *Ennio Marchetto, Saucy Jack and The Space Vixens, The Oxygen Project, Fecund Theatre* and *Mel and Sue.*

## Tom Cotterill – Company Stage Manager

Tom read English and Theatre Arts at Goldsmiths', specialising in Scenography. Technical and Stage management credits include *The Chimp that Spoke* (David Glass Ensemble), *The Secret Life of Swift and Gulliver* (Group K), *Sealboy: Freak* (Mat Fraser), *I Am the Walrus* (Nabil Shaban), *Walking amongst Sleepers* (Caroline Parker) and, through association with Oval House Theatre, *Cardboard Citizens, The Dende Collective* (The Piranha Lounge), *The Barber of Seville* (Garden Opera Company) and *Angie La Mar.* Production and Set Design credits include *Talking about Men* and *Juniors Story* (Oval House Theatre), *Sacrificed* (Spirit2Reality), *Coming up for Air* (Crescent Theatre) and *Under their Influence* (Kushite Theatre Company). Further creative collaboration with Theatre Buddha / Illpalchettostage (The Canterville Ghost ) and for Group K.

## Heidi Riley –Technical Stage Manager

Trained at the Royal Scottish Academy of Music and Drama in Technical Stage Management. Worked freelance in Scotland for companies including The Citizens Theatre, Scottish Opera, The Tramway and also completed two seasons at Pitlochry Festival Theatre. Touring Companies include 7:84 Theatre Scotland, Grey Coast Theatre Company, Anatomy Dance, Tag Theatre Company and the David Gayle Company. In 2000 started working for The Royal Court Theatre in the Lighting Department. After two years left to travel for a year and now back in London as a freelancer.

## Nick Manning – Sound Effects

Nick trained in Stage Management at The Central School of Speech and Drama. He is currently working as the sound technician at The Lyric Hammersmith, London. Recent productions include: *Great Expectations* (Bristol Old Vic), *Camille, A Christmas Carol, Island of Slaves, The Prince of Homburg, Aladdin, The Servant, Pinocchio, The White Devil, The Threesome* (Lyric Hammersmith), *Out of our Heads – Susan and Janice* (ATC and Edinburgh Fringe 2002). Previously Nick worked at Derby Playhouse and The Gordon Craig Theatre where productions include *The Wizard of Oz* and *Godspell.* He is currently working on sound designs for The Lyric Hammersmith and The Bush. *Rabbit* is Nick's first collaboration with Frantic Assembly.

**frantic**
*assembly*

Frantic Assembly was founded in 1994 by Artistic Directors Scott Graham and Steven Hoggett, and Administrative Director Vicki Middleton.
**'Frantic Assembly have their fingers on the collective pulse of a generation'** The Times
Renowned both nationally and internationally for attracting new, young audiences, Frantic Assembly stand at the forefront of new British physical theatre. Frantic has established itself as one of the most innovative and exciting companies around, touring extensively throughout the UK including a pioneering West End run in 1999. Five time recipients of *Time Out Critics Choice*, the company also received a *Time Out Live Award* for *Sell Out* in 1998. To date, Frantic have presented their work in almost thirty countries worldwide, and are studied at GCSE, 'A' and Degree level throughout Britain.

The key to this success lies with the intention and nature of the work. Frantic produces intelligent, relevant theatre, which engages, excites and energises audiences with a style firmly rooted in contemporary culture. The themes of the work are drawn from everyday life, attitudes and practices. The intention is to bring about an understanding of people's experience, behaviour and environment, in a way that is accessible and stimulating.

Frantic's work had been described as **'the bleeding edge of contemporary British Theatre'** (The Stage), **'Theatre of the twenty-first century'** (The Guardian), **'Crucial viewing for anyone interested in the future of theatre'** (Time Out).
**'One of the most compelling and consistently innovative companies currently working in British Theatre…Frantic continues to break the mould'** The Stage
Following huge successes with *Look Back in Anger* (1994), *Klub* (1995), *Flesh* (1996) and *Zero* (1997), Frantic recent credits include award winning *Sell Out* (1998), *Hymns* (1999), *Underworld* (2000), *Tiny Dynamite* (2001), *Heavenly* (2002) and their first mid scale show *Peepshow* (2002).

Frantic Assembly
BAC, Lavender Hill
London SW11 5TF
Tel / Fax 020 7228 8885
Email: Vicki@franticassembly.co.uk
www.franticassembly.co.uk

An education pack *A Teachers Guide to Rabbit* is available for free from 22 September. Go to www.franticassembly.co.uk and click on the education page to download.

# DRUM THEATRE PLYMOUTH

The Drum Theatre Plymouth is a theatre of origination, producing new writing, physical theatre and other innovative work for Plymouth and the South-West. As a part of the Theatre Royal Plymouth complex, it has become a leading force in the national development of writing, directing and producing relationships.

Recent premieres have included EDWARD GANT'S AMAZING FEATS OF LONELINESS by Anthony Neilson, THE GREEN MAN by Doug Lucie, subsequently produced at the Bush Theatre, London and MR. PLACEBO by Isabel Wright in a collaboration with the Traverse Theatre, Edinburgh.

In addition to RABBIT which extends our long-term relationship with Frantic Assembly, our current autumn programme includes Gregory Burke's highly acclaimed THE STRAITS in a co-production with Paines Plough and Hampstead Theatre and Emma Frost's new play AIRSICK in co-production with the Bush.

We also present the latest works from GRAEAE, TOLD BY AN IDIOT and THE ROYAL COURT, THE RED ROOM and OUT OF JOINT, as well as a popular, annual Christmas residency from POP-UP.

This year has seen the official opening of TR2 - Europe's first purpose-built Production and Education Centre - on a waterfront site in Plymouth. This award-winning structure provides unrivalled creative, construction, rehearsal and education facilities as well as becoming a cultural focus for the people of the South West.

**Simon Stokes**
Artistic Director

www.theatreroyal.com

Chief Executive **Adrian Vinken**
Artistic Director **Simon Stokes**
General Manager **Alan Finch**
Technical Director **Ed Wilson**

" **The Drum Theatre Plymouth, a theatre with increasingly big ideas, is staking its claim with new found confidence.**"
The Guardian

# LAKESIDE ARTS CENTRE

# A VIBRANT AND DIVERSE VENUE SITUATED IN IDYLLIC SURROUNDINGS AT THE UNIVERSITY OF NOTTINGHAM

**DJANOGLY ART GALLERY**
Nationally renowned for its exhibition programme which ranges from major historical shows to groundbreaking contemporary installations.

**WALLNER GALLERY**
Providing a platform for the work of local and regional artists and also the venue for informal lunchtime talks, preview nights and special Lakeside events.

**WESTON GALLERY**
A public showcase for The University of Nottingham's prized and unique manuscripts collections.

**DJANOGLY RECITAL HALL**
One of the UK's best compact concert halls, often used by BBC Radio 3 for recording and broadcasting. Superb acoustics along with an informal ambience provide the ideal setting for a varied range of music from chamber recitals to cutting edge contemporary compositions.

**DJANOGLY THEATRE**
Hosts a stunning programme of visiting contemporary drama, dance, comedy, jazz and world music, as well as literary events and foreign language film screenings. The programme of theatre for the under 7's has established itself as some of the best in the region and Lakeside's first in-house production, *Krapp's Last Tape*, starring Kenneth Alan Taylor received critical acclaim prior to embarking on a national tour. Djanogly Theatre is also home to the regional festivals NOTT Dance and NOW.

For information contact the Box Office on **0115 846 7777** or email **lakeside-marketing@nottingham.ac.uk**

LAKESIDE

 The University of Nottingham

# Directors' Notes

In the past, Frantic shows were normally born out of conversations between ourselves as to what concerned us at a particular point in our lives. For this project, it was our intention to set ourselves a new challenge and search for an existing play that we could then Franticise. After many dark, autumnal months of relentless script reading and no result, we decided to take a break and resume our search in the new year.

As is often the case with Frantic, results came up when we least expected it. A stroll past the Griffin Theatre in Sydney and a particularly eye-catching poster lead to our discovery of Brendan Cowell's *Rabbit* which was due to premiere in Australia.

Reading *Rabbit* was a profound experience. As a creative team, our normal practise was to talk about how we felt and then look to create a script from these ideas. With *Rabbit*, we found a play that contained and explored ideas that we hadn't realised had been trapped in our heads. Events over the last two years have very much challenged and redefined our understanding and experience of the term 'family'. We found this play remarkable in its bravery, its unflinching commitment to exposing the darker parts of our personalities. As a play, it contained so much and yet afforded us the opportunity to create, both physically and directorially, with the delicate and complex 'spaces' that exist between the five characters.

The bravery of the play has been matched in every way by Brendan and the cast. Brendan's willingness and desire to experiment is complemented by a brilliant cast whose energy, creativity and trust has and is creating a rehearsal process that is inspirational for us. The skill and generosity of the creative team assembled here has meant that working on something like this has only ever been a joy. For that – thanks. Spex to you all...

As for the rest of you – we hope this play hurts and heals in equal measure.

Scott Graham and Steven Hoggett
August 2003

P.S. Yeah, we can't believe there's an interval either...

# Writer's Notes

I wrote *Rabbit* in 2001 when I realised my father had cancer.

He was lucky enough to survive. But the fear of loss inspired me to write a play about dysfunctional family, whose true salvation comes only in the face of mortality. I'm beyond excited to see this very personal play touch a larger audience, in the hands of the frantically wonderful Frantic Assembly and this great cast and production team.

In Australia talkback radio is a national phenomenon. A handful of men, between the hours of six and nine am bark their beliefs down the airwaves, and hence, control the politics and views of a large percentage of the people.

Their views, unfortunately, are myopic and closed.

*Rabbit* takes Paul Cave, a hybrid form of these 'shock jocks', and plonks him at the end of his life, realising too late the futility of opinion, and the importance of family love.

Brendan Cowell
August 2003

# RABBIT

First published in 2003 by Oberon Books Ltd.
(incorporating Absolute Classics)
521 Caledonian Road, London N7 9RH
Tel: 020 7607 3637 / Fax: 020 7607 3629

e-mail: oberon.books@btinternet.com
www.oberonbooks.com

A catalogue record for this book is available from the British
Library.

ISBN: 1 84002 394 5

Cover image: '*Untitled: What makes certain*' by John Isaccs.
By kind permission of the 20:21 Gallery.
Design by emma@chamberlainmcauley.co.uk

Printed in Great Britain by Antony Rowe Ltd, Chippenham.

# Characters

PAUL CAVE

MADELINE CAVE

SPIN

KATE CAVE

DRIVER

*Light.*

*Holiday House on top of a mountain. Glass walls. Open plan living.*

*MADELINE stands eyes closed, breathing calmly. She is dressed according to her interests.*

*SPIN enters, holding a pack.*

SPIN: Ah. Baby?

MADELINE: Yes, my baby?

SPIN: Where's the best place?

MADELINE: In my heart baby.

SPIN: No, like the best place.

MADELINE: In my heart baby.

SPIN: No like the best place to do the –

MADELINE: To do the what?

SPIN: To do the 'uh'! –

MADELINE: To 'uh'! What?

SPIN: To you know? 'Uh'!

MADELINE: To 'uh'!?

    *Pause.*

    Oh, okay, 'uh'.

SPIN: Yeah.

MADELINE: To fuck or shoot up – ?

SPIN: Shoot up. Shoot up.

MADELINE: (*Disappointed.*) Oh. 'Uh'.

SPIN: To shoot up then fuck baby. Shoot up then fuck.

MADELINE: That's better.

SPIN: Where baby? Fucken' where?

MADELINE: They won't be here for an hour you can just do it in here.

SPIN: Cool. Hmmm.

MADELINE: What?

*MADELINE touches him, he spins away.*

What?!

SPIN: What about if I go on the nod baby. If I just fucken' nod and your olds walk in and I've got my head in the friggin' potpourri. Like fuck that.

MADELINE: Let 'em see. I don't care. I'll wake you with a salacious entrée of fellatio and Long Island ice tea right in front of them –

SPIN: Ohh – tempting – but dunno. Still a bit wrong. Like friggin' the Jesus dude up here on the wall. Respect for the marvels baby. For the carpenter.

MADELINE: Laundry? The laundry is sterile and dark.

*SPIN paces.*

SPIN: Dangerous though babe. I could fall asleep in the front loader. Inhale detergent. Get caught in the spin cycle. Dangerous shit.

MADELINE: Heroin isn't dangerous at all?

SPIN: No, it's just famous baby. Where baby where fuck!?

MADELINE: In the bedroom.

*MADELINE touches him. SPIN spins away.*

SPIN: There's bunks baby. I'll relapse into childhood and come out the wrong end. I can't afford the therapy.

MADELINE: I'll pay for your therapy baby.

SPIN: Oh, baby. (*Panic.*) Where else?!

*SPIN jumps up and down.*

MADELINE: On the roof –

SPIN: Warmer – Closer – Better – Nature. But the breeze baby. Reports predict a southerly bluster.

MADELINE: Kitchen?

SPIN: Ahhhhhhh! – Nah. It's not a domestic drug baby.

MADELINE: Bathroom?

SPIN: I'll O D baby. Like in the movies. Fuck that. Bathroom's a curse.

*SPIN jumps harder and harder, stomping his legs hard onto the floor.*

MADELINE: Okay ah – In the hallway, between the first bedroom and the kitchen. Little bit of childhood. Little bit –

SPIN: Of domesticity! Perfect blend.

*SPIN barrels out.*

MADELINE: Baby?

*Almost.*

SPIN: Yep?

*Pause.*

Yes baby?

MADELINE: Come here.

SPIN: But babe –

MADELINE: Come here.

*They meet. MADELINE is kissing him hard. SPIN shuddering.*

SPIN: I gotta cook baby.

MADELINE: I know.

*MADELINE kissing harder. Grind.*

SPIN: Baby I gotta cook I gotta cook –

MADELINE: I know.

SPIN: Baby –

MADELINE: Yes you have to –

SPIN: Cook. I gotta cook.

MADELINE: Yeah. Aw – ?

*Clench broken.*

SPIN: Baby fuck!

MADELINE: I'm not. I'm just –

SPIN: You know the shit I do.

MADELINE: I know but it's just, well my parents –

SPIN: Baby, I can't relate just from the chin. Like off the cuff. I'm from another world. 'Worldz'. Different worlds.

MADELINE: We relate.

SPIN: Yeah but we're the same person baby. We got the soul of the city. Ahhh.

*SPIN is shaking all over.*

MADELINE: My parents may be from a different world, but they're just as scared as you are.

SPIN: What do they have to be scared of? Look at this place. The toilet has a motorbike in it.

MADELINE: It's a sculpture.

SPIN: What?

MADELINE: It's a sculpture of a motorbike. It's not an actual motorbike.

SPIN: Well exactly. What is there to be scared of when the motorbike isn't even a motorbike?

*They look at each other. Close.*

Don't puppy the eyes Madeline. This is my thing.

MADELINE: Just an hour. Just do an hour in the room with them sharp, and if you're bursting then go whack it in.

SPIN: But baby –

MADELINE: I know what you do, and of course I wouldn't be here if I didn't recognise its purpose for you. But baby, this is a –

SPIN: Hey! I'm a chameleon baby.

*They kiss.*

MADELINE: Go shoot up then ya pathetic junkie.

SPIN: Cool baby.

MADELINE: Whatever.

*SPIN dives out with the pack. He speaks from the hallway off.*

*MADELINE applies natural make-up.*

SPIN: You want a hit baby?

MADELINE: What do you think?! Of course I fucking do. I'm eating my own heart out. But I think tonight, tonight I choose to greet my parents awake.

SPIN: Very traditional choice.

MADELINE: But later, when the futility of blood relations kicks in and they've drunk all the pinot noir and collapsed. Later, I'll put some in for sure.

SPIN: Cool baby. So run me through this fiasco. They've never wanted to meet me before.

MADELINE: It was Dad's idea. Feels he's losing touch with what's 'real'. Wants to 'vibe down' with the young people.

SPIN: What's 'vibe down' mean? Like play Twister or something?

MADELINE: It's dad trying to be youth colloquial. Drink red wine and discuss 'irony'. Mum'll just flit round the kitchen guzzling plonk and stating the obvious, and dad will play all cryptic and bitter.

*SPIN takes his hit from off.*

SPIN: Ohhhhhh.......

MADELINE: Oh. Yeah. But you know I don't want to be just atypical cynic on the set up. Like just because I'm a young person. We should embrace the efforts my parents are making to bridge the gulf and look into their eyes and ask them what it used to be like – when they were our age. And things were harder. And there was no hypertext. And YMCAs were exciting halls. And people faced each other when they danced. You were home by ten. We should embrace that.

SPIN: – Serious?

MADELINE: God no! I haven't the faintest why they want this spontaneous weekend in the hills. Dad only calls me to check on the car and mum only calls for cosmetic advice. I don't know. That's the truth of it. I don't know and I don't really care. I'm just going to give them the update and watch them spin –

*SPIN enters. Whacked.*

SPIN: I'm with you baby. I'm into it. Let's bridge shit.

MADELINE: Dad. Mum. This is my boyfriend Spin. He's a hip-hop artist and a chef. He makes me feel alive when I'm with him and I want to spend the rest of my life in arm's reach of him. Do you think I've made a good decision? Definitely better than that upstanding young man Clint from the Ski Club. Worlds apart. He may not be able to see you or shake your hand, for he's just reduced serotonin, a vital neurotransmitter in the brain, to almost nothing, and, in turn, activated all his opioid receptors so he's in a honey cloud right now, but believe me, this boy rocks my world, and one day, will make a wonderful father.

SPIN: Super. Got beer?

MADELINE: Only Belgian.

*MADELINE points in the direction of the beer.*

SPIN: Belgian beer. Super.

*SPIN moves to bar fridge. Removes a long Belgian beer.*

Wow!

Baby I'm into this. Bonding with the elders. I care.

MADELINE: You care about the devil on a jet ski that's firing through your blood stream. The rest is icing. You don't care.

SPIN: I care baby. I care more than you can see.

MADELINE: How do you know what I can see?

SPIN: My parents man. If I had the opportunity.

MADELINE: I know baby. Sorry.

SPIN: Totally. Totes.

*SPIN opens his beer. Knocks back a quantity.*

What was I saying?

MADELINE: You were talking about your parents.

*Pause.*

And if you had the opportunity.

SPIN: My parents man. If I could spend like a weekend of Belgian beer and vibe with them, in such a nice, florid bitch of a holiday retreat like this one. I'd give my left arm.

MADELINE: You just did…

SPIN: Huh? Oh, very funny. You're very very funny my darling Madeline.

*He moves up behind her.*

But not as funny as you are sexy.

*He spins her around. Kiss. Hold.*

MADELINE: And you're not as fucked up as you are cute.

SPIN: And I'm pretty fucked up.

MADELINE: As they come.

SPIN: Large. Come sit in the clouds with me.

MADELINE: Don't.

SPIN: It's good baby, it's really good. It's all honey and sparks.

MADELINE: Why can't you just see that I'm trying not to want something and support me through that?

SPIN: Why can't you just see that I know where the good cloud is and help me put you on it?

*Kiss. Kiss again. Kissing. Looking.*

MADELINE: Honey.

SPIN: And sparks.

*Kissing.*

MADELINE: What about my parents –

*Kiss.*

Fuck 'em!

SPIN: That's my Bitch!

*Kiss. Kids let loose.*

*Black.*

*Light.*

*MADELINE and SPIN are unconscious, sprawled half-dressed on the floor. An expressive mess of young people's things beside them. Spilt drinks, belongings, drugs, syringes, clothing, et cetera.*

*A large man in a uniform stands in the doorway. This is DRIVER. He lowers two overnight bags.*

DRIVER: Madeline Cave.

*No movement.*

Madeline Cave.

*No movement. DRIVER uses his big booming voice.*

Madeline Cave!

*SPIN jolts to life.*

SPIN: Who the fuck are you? Did you take my shit? I don't owe you nothing. I'm a chef, and a hip-hop artist.

DRIVER: Spin is it?

25

SPIN: How did you know that? What is this?

DRIVER: My name is Driver –

*SPIN picks up the syringe. Points it at DRIVER.*

SPIN: Stand back motherfucker I'm warning you. This wand is full packed up with the death of the city. A to Zee of hepatitis dude and that's just the tip of the berg. Word! One more step and you got that for life. I'm carrying it all man, you name it. And I'll pop this in you. I'll pop you man. No fear in me doing that. I got it in me to kill shit. Totally. Totes.

DRIVER: My name is Driver. I am permanent personal driver to Mr and Mrs Cave, your party partner's parents, who own the house in which she is currently sprawled, who are approaching this very doorway bearing bags from Jones the Grocer, Vintage Cellars, and a box from the Rabbit Farm. I suggest you do away with all evidence of delinquency and knock some life into our dear Madeline before her very powerful parents panic and punish accordingly.

SPIN: Have I got time to think about this?

DRIVER: Ten seconds.

SPIN: Shit fuck.

*SPIN gets to work. DRIVER takes view, rolling the bags into the bedrooms.*

DRIVER: They're on the Asian pebbling. Approaching water feature. Passing the elephant hedge. Three seconds.

*We hear PAUL and KATE approaching in a squabble.*

Two!

*SPIN has picked up the needles, clothes, and stuff, and slammed them into a nap sack. He drapes MADELINE over his shoulder and carries her out.*

26

And…

*DRIVER magically prepares the house.*

One!

*Just as he completes KATE enters holding groceries excitedly, followed by PAUL, who holds a box containing a rabbit.*

*DRIVER notices the spilt beer and leaps to stand in front of it.*

KATE: Darling! Yoo hoo! Is that you? Squirrel?

PAUL: You tell 'em we were here?

DRIVER: I – no.

PAUL: Did you yell out?

KATE: Darling? Yoo hoo! Is that you? Squirrel?

DRIVER: No, Sir. I mean. Yes Sir. I did yell.

PAUL: What did you yell?

DRIVER: I yelled –

*The sound of a shower.*

KATE: Darling! Yoo hoo! Is that –

PAUL: She's in the shower Kate. Let her wash.

KATE: I'm just excited Paul. I'm just excited. Is that illegal? Cucumbers.

*KATE sets down the cucumber into a section.*

PAUL: So they're here and that's that. Can you express to me their demeanour Driver?

DRIVER: Jovial Sir.

KATE: Radishes and carrots.

*KATE puts the radishes and carrots down in a section.*

PAUL: Jovial?

DRIVER: They seemed – relaxed Sir.

PAUL: Indulged?

DRIVER: Well, young. Slipshod –

PAUL: Don't waffle Driver.

DRIVER: Sorry Sir –

PAUL: And my daughter.

KATE: Lettuces and cabbages.

*KATE sets down lettuces and cabbages in a section.*

PAUL: Did my daughter look – happy?

KATE: Darling! Yoo Hoo! Is that you? Squirrel?

DRIVER: Yes Sir. Quite at home Sir. She really is a princess Sir.

PAUL: Hmmm. And the boy. Ethnic? Clean shaven?

DRIVER: He looked just fine Sir. Full of beans.

KATE: French beans.

*KATE sets down French beans in a section.*

*PAUL sets down the rabbit box.*

DRIVER: Now Sir –

PAUL: It's nebulous these days isn't it Driver? 'These days.' It's gone beyond racism. You just can't trust any culture. A different culture reflects a different system of dangers. Faith is a munition. Wouldn't you say Driver?

DRIVER: They seemed jovial Sir.

PAUL: Splurged?

DRIVER: Wanton.

PAUL: Lost?

DRIVER: Sybaritic.

PAUL: I said don't go on Driver.

DRIVER: Sir. Apologies.

*KATE slams the bench.*

KATE: We forgot the fucking parsley!

*Rabbit flutters in the box.*

Where shall I put the rabbit?

PAUL: Just leave it there for the time being now. We'll kill it in a minute.

KATE: I don't know why we just don't buy them dead and stripped from the butcher.

PAUL: Did they seem to have a good connection – the boy and my daughter?

DRIVER: Yes Sir. Quite a rhythm and rhyme with each other Sir. They seemed. To have. In the brief glimpse I managed to get of them Sir –

PAUL: Did you get a look at them or not Driver?

DRIVER: I must say no Sir.

PAUL: Yes or no Driver?

DRIVER: I must say no Sir.

PAUL: So, it's a no Driver?

DRIVER: Well, yes and no, Sir. In a scurry to the bathroom.

PAUL: Why were they scurrying?

KATE: Paul, you're not at work now. They were scurrying. We used to scurry. It's not illegal.

PAUL: Mmm. Alright. You can go back to the car now Driver.

DRIVER: Sir, I was going to ask you –

PAUL: What? I'm not at work.

DRIVER: Sorry Sir.

KATE: What is it Driver? Paul.

*KATE gestures to PAUL.*

*PAUL extracts a note.*

PAUL: Here's fifty, now go back to the car.

DRIVER: I don't want the fifty Sir.

PAUL: Well what the fuck do you want?

KATE: Paul. Language.

DRIVER: Sir, my baby boy turns one tonight. One year old. And he's sick. Hospital. And I was just wondering –

KATE: I didn't know you were a father Driver.

DRIVER: Yes, Ma'am.

KATE: Oh how gorgeous. When did you become a father?

DRIVER: A year ago tonight Ma'am.

KATE: Oh, of course.

PAUL: Did I give you the night off? One year ago?

DRIVER: No, Sir.

PAUL: Hmm, how far away is the hospital Driver?

DRIVER: Fifty minutes Sir. Forty-five with luck.

PAUL: Fifty.

KATE: Just let him go Paul.

PAUL: Just unpack Kate I'm thinking.

KATE: It's not illegal to want to see your sick child Paul. It's not illegal.

PAUL: Unpack Kate. Unpack.

KATE: I have unpacked. Everything but the blasted rabbit.

*Rabbit flutter.*

DRIVER: My son's first birthday Sir. He's very sick.

PAUL: I heard you Driver. No need to pluck the heart strings. I'm hearing you.

DRIVER: I'll keep my pager on my hip and be here within the hour at your request Sir.

PAUL: I'm just trying to comprehend the logic of having a driver, a 'permanent' driver, paying for that service, of permanence –

KATE: Oh, Paul. He's just going to sit in the car all night anyway.

PAUL: Beside the point it's a matter of definition. What is there without definition? Mess. War. Imbroglio. I'm not immoral or malicious or cruel by no means am I cruel but I am a believer in definition. 'Permanent' driver. Permanent. If you were a 'casual' driver or a 'within the hour' driver or 'when I feel like having a bit of a drive' driver I may. What time does your child go under Driver?

DRIVER: Between seven and eight Sir.

PAUL: It's seven now Driver. You'd catch his last round of rapid eye movement and then –

*PAUL makes the disappearing 'poof' noise.*

Who wants to spend their night observing a sedated kid? Maudlin. You can call the wife on my phone if you like but there will be no obstruction of the term permanent. 'Definition.'

DRIVER: 'Definition.' Yes, Sir.

PAUL: Would you like to use the phone to call Driver?

DRIVER: I have my own in the car, Sir.

PAUL: Oh, you do? A cellular phone?

DRIVER: Yes, Sir.

PAUL: Is that mine?

DRIVER: Yes, Sir. You gave it to me to use.

PAUL: Do I pay that bill?

DRIVER: Yes, Sir.

PAUL: And you use that to make private calls?

DRIVER: Yes Sir. No Sir. Some Sir.

PAUL: But it's mine?

DRIVER: It's a separate sim Sir, but yes Sir, your account Sir.

PAUL: Well go on then. Tell your wife you love her.

KATE: How sweet. Ohh.

PAUL: And don't be down Driver, you have the rest of your life with the child, the human brain doesn't recall anything till its third phase, you have years of loose time. Enjoy. Go on. Back to your car.

DRIVER: That's the thing Sir. I'm not sure if he will –

PAUL: Drivers sit in cars.

DRIVER: Sir, it's my son – !

32

KATE: Oh, baby boy.

PAUL: They sit in cars. Drivers. Sit in cars.

*DRIVER takes a moment. Leaves.*

Oh Kate don't give me your catholic guilt if I make single acts of allowance then the world will slowly fall apart. I must be stoic when it comes to definition.

KATE: It's not definition I'm perturbed by. It's irony.

PAUL: 'Irony.' 'Irony.' Everyone's talking about 'irony'.

KATE: Well darling you make this big fuss about spending time with your child, after twenty or so years of being relatively invisible –

PAUL: Invisible – i.e. busy, i.e. seditious, i.e. prolific, i.e. 'the voice of the real world', i.e. without 'irony'.

KATE: There's 'irony' in your sudden flash of paternity, your sudden need to gather closeness with your child, and then you stand there and deny a fellow father access to his own sick child. Now, that's irony.

PAUL: Hmmm. Yes, well. If it wasn't for my 'irony' then we wouldn't be standing on this heated floor in a glass house on top of a mountain about to enjoy the beauty of baked rabbit and vintage pinot noir. Irony is a children's toy. Success is sacrifice.

KATE: I'll just pop down and tell Driver to go –

*KATE moves to the door.*

PAUL: I may need him Kate!

*KATE stops.*

Did you ever think that?

KATE: Oh.

*Rabbit flutter.*

Any ideas on the death of that rabbit, the fluttering in the box is unnerving me?

PAUL: Time should kill it. No! Let's bake it alive!

KATE: Paul.

*KATE goes to pick up the spilt beer.*

PAUL: Leave it.

KATE: No.

*PAUL instructs her to leave it without speaking, she obeys.*

*Shower off.*

Shower's off.

PAUL: Oh, it is too. Well observed.

KATE: Stop it –

PAUL: Darling there's a roof on the house. Darling I was hungry before I ate dinner. Now I'm not. Gee, it'll be hot when that sun comes out. Isn't the road black?

KATE: Make me a drink before I punch you.

*They stop. Smile at each other.*

PAUL: Making you a drink. That's what I'm going to do. Darling, I'm walking to the bar, and I'm opening the cabinet, I'm extracting the liquor and closing the cabinet door.

KATE: I could kill you sometimes.

PAUL: Well there's no need to now is there?

*Hair dryer screams to life from off.*

KATE: Ooh, that's a –

PAUL: Hair dryer. Yes, I know. I've seen them. They dry hair. Sometimes people put them in baths and turn them on. Thank you dear.

*PAUL hands her a drink. She playfully prods him.*

KATE: Are you not going to have a drink?

PAUL: I will I will. I want to have my first drink with my daughter.

KATE: And her new boyfriend.

PAUL: Her new boyfriend. Yes. The new boyfriend. The boy that scurries.

*Rabbit flutter.*

KATE: Darling.

PAUL: Yes, my dear –

KATE: Are you sure you're okay to tell her. I can do it for you.

PAUL: No –

KATE: I think it'd be best to just say it right now. Just get it out of the way.

PAUL: In my own time.

KATE: No darling I really think you should just get in there and announce it as soon as she steps out with the boy. She's going to need the time to assimilate –

PAUL: I'll tell her when it feels right.

KATE: But –

PAUL: There will be a right time.

KATE: Sure, but –

PAUL: There will be a right time!

*KATE comforts PAUL.*

KATE: Just tell her now darl. Let's not dilly-dally round. Best to just do it I think. Get it out there and over with.

PAUL: It's my fate, Kate.

KATE: I'll tell her.

PAUL: No you will not. I will do the telling. In my own time.

KATE: But darling –

PAUL: In my own time.

KATE: But –

PAUL: In my own time.

KATE: But time isn't really of the –

*KATE searches for the end of the sentence. Realises it makes no sense.*

Okay dear.

PAUL: What's the boys name again?

KATE: Who?

*SPIN enters.*

PAUL: The new boyfriend. The scurrying – ?

SPIN: Spin Sir. My name's Spin.

*Pause.*

PAUL: How do you expect me to react to that?

SPIN: Sorry, Sir?

PAUL: Spin? Spin? How do you expect me to react to that?

SPIN: I'm not sure Sir. It's just my name.

36

PAUL: Are your parents musicians?

SPIN: No, Sir. They weren't.

PAUL: Oh, I do apologise. They're late?

SPIN: Late, yeah. Dead.

KATE: (*Remembering.*) Ooh yes of course! Oh. Darling would you like a drink? A beer?

SPIN: Oh, thanks Mrs Cave, ahhh, Ma'am, ahh, I would very much like to do that. I did, admittedly, I, ah, have had a beer already, I had a Belgian beer earlier.

PAUL: The one tipped over on the floor here Spin?

SPIN: Oh shit. Um. Sorry. Yes.

*SPIN picks up the beer.*

PAUL: There's a bin in the laundry. For bottles.

SPIN: Sorry Sir. I'm not usually like this I really aren't.

PAUL: No?

*SPIN looks at PAUL. A moment.*

SPIN: No.

*SPIN disappears to the laundry.*

KATE: You having fun Paul? Having fun?

PAUL: Oh, it's just play.

KATE: The poor boy's parents are dead! No more play!

*SPIN enters.*

SPIN: Oh that's cool Mrs Cave, my parents being dead isn't like a huge thing anymore. I've totally like moved through all that ey, like yeah it's still fucked that they crashed and died but I'm totally like all new and repaired of the first grief loss fucked parts –

37

KATE: Oh, grief yes. Grief is very big isn't it?

SPIN: Big?

KATE: Grief yes. The grieving. The 'grief' of it all.

SPIN: Yeah, it's a big part of it – is that what you meant?

KATE: Oh yes and it was a car crash Madeline tells me! They died in a car crash yes? In a car?

SPIN: Ah, no. Light aeroplane.

KATE: That's it yes. Light aeroplane. That's simply terrible!

SPIN: Yeah, no it's not that good. Like I wasn't like stoked at the time it happened. But I've totally made it through 'grief' wise. And no longer even hold it as a power source or anything. It's just a shit thing that happened. So I guess I'm saying like don't feel like you have to tread lightly or anything. I'm not like about to crumble or fuck out or nothin'. Totes.

PAUL: Have you had any reactions to the grief? Insecurity? Paranoia? Drug addiction? Popularity?

SPIN: Ah, no. Pretty smooth glide out.

KATE: Mind the pun.

SPIN: Oh, yes. Nice one Mrs Cave!

*SPIN laughs.*

PAUL: 'Cos it's boring, drug addiction. Seeking false refuge in the caves of high. Especially heroin. As a drug – tenacious, seductive. As a friend – greedy. You start using it to warm the soul. Heat the heart. But I'll tell you this from any distance Spin. It always ends up owning you. Controlling you. I don't care who you are. Grief is such a cheap ticket.

SPIN: I really couldn't agree – more, Sir.

*Rabbit flutter.*

PAUL: Did you shower with my daughter Spin?

SPIN: Sorry Sir?

KATE: Paul! No more!

PAUL: Kate pointed out earlier in another acute observation that the shower was on. Did you shower with her? Or did she shower alone?

SPIN: Ah, you really want me to answer this question Sir?

PAUL: I didn't ask it to hear my voice out loud.

SPIN: No, you're probably sick to death of your own voice. I mean – with 'The Real World'.

PAUL: I understand.

SPIN: Well, dude it's a pretty weird thing to ask ey –

KATE: It's off Paul. It's simply off.

SPIN: I mean it's just a shower. Like, a place of cleaning.

PAUL: I know what a shower is. I have one every morning. I disrobe, I enter the desired Celsius, and I scrub. I often shampoo. Rarely condition. Why does hair require a condition? Hair's condition is that it is hair. I body wash.

SPIN: We body wash too. Mad prefers it to soap. We make our own all-natural paw paw body wash.

KATE: Oh.

PAUL: So you do shower with my daughter?

KATE: Paul.

PAUL: Oh, Kate just admit you kind of want to know now too. Shower for two?

SPIN: Yes, Sir. Strike me down. I shower with Madeline.

PAUL: Thank you for your honesty. You're doing very well.

SPIN: It's practical Sir. Like we don't embellish. It's more ritualistic than anything. We just wash each other and get out. It's Eastern. We don't embellish it.

PAUL: Eastern. Okay. Okay. Hmm. Beer?

SPIN: Yes, Sir.

PAUL: If you promise to keep this one upright Spin?

SPIN: Ha. Yes, Sir.

*PAUL moves to the bar.*

*MADELINE enters.*

MADELINE: I'm here.

KATE: Darling!

*KATE almost falls over.*

You look – effulgent. Glowing. What cleanser are you using?

MADELINE: We make our own.

KATE: Oh, how resourceful.

MADELINE: Spin and I have a paw-paw crop hanging off the balcony of the flat. We make soap, cleansers, candles, bath bombs –

*KATE interrupts.*

KATE: Hmm, how tiresome!

MADELINE: Better than the chemically corrupted bullshit you pump into your skull.

KATE: Botox is harmless darling. You should come to one of the parties.

MADELINE: Harmless? It's paralysis.

KATE: Darling, I can't just slap a piece of fruit on my head and maintain the image of youth. I'm an aging woman. With aging lines. That calls for a much more industrial approach.

MADELINE: It's not about image mum.

KATE: It fades darling. Like a power ballad. It fades.

MADELINE: You're disarming your source of expression.

KATE: Read my aura.

MADELINE: Your head's going to implode.

KATE: Yours is going to turn green and sprout.

MADELINE: Whatever.

KATE: Let's not fight. Let's drink some wine. Paul?

PAUL: We were just talking to Spin about his dead parents and the virtues of Eastern bathing rituals.

MADELINE: Oh, fabulous.

KATE: I thought they died in a car crash but it was actually a light aeroplane.

MADELINE: Do you prefer that?

KATE: Well, no. But yes. Much more. Much less visible. Car crashes are so – public! So –

MADELINE: On the road?

KATE: Yes. Exactly!

*PAUL gives SPIN a beer.*

PAUL: Spin was also telling us that you shower together.

MADELINE: Was he?

SPIN: Well I didn't like, volunteer it, but –

PAUL: What was your old boyfriend's name?

MADELINE: Dad.

KATE: Paul.

SPIN: – Clint?

PAUL: Clint. Yes, that's right Spin. Did you shower with Clint?

SPIN: Me?

KATE: Oh. Oh, I did like Clint. Clint was a lovely boy. Head of the Ski Club. Very clean-cut. Polite.

PAUL: But not the type you'd shower with?

KATE: Well he was very clean.

MADELINE: Is this going to be it Dad? Cryptic games? Sharp digs and tickles? If it is tell me 'cos I'll drink a litre of vodka to warm me up for the clever-dicking.

PAUL: Clint never struck me as the type you'd shower with. Clint was – Clint was –

MADELINE: Clint was obsessive compulsive okay Paul. He washed his hands in the sink fifteen times an hour. So no, we didn't shower with each other. Someone make me a vodka martini. Now!

SPIN: Yes, I was just going to ask you Mr Cave. With my beer. You gave it to me with the lid still on, is that some code to not open it or something? I'm just trying to gather the meaning of that.

PAUL: I respect your curiosity Spin. And yes, as I stated to my wife prior to your entrance my intention was to share my first drink with my daughter –

KATE: And her new boyfriend.

PAUL: And her new boyfriend.

SPIN: Cool. That's me right? So –

*PAUL hands SPIN an opening utensil.*

PAUL: So whilst I prepare my freshly-washed daughter with a vodka martini feel free to release the lid on your Belgian beer and we will meet back here in the centre of the room in just a moment for a clinking of the glasses and the virginal gulp. Now that's Eastern.

*PAUL begins to fix.*

KATE: Oh, you must forgive him Spin. He tends to make sections and concepts out of everything. He thinks he's on air the whole time you see.

PAUL: They call it the future fifteen minutes in radio Spin. Always let your listener know what's coming up in the next fifteen minutes so they become hooked subconsciously, and stay tuned. The same applies to life Spin. We always want to know what's about to happen, never what's happening now.

MADELINE: And what the fuck is happening now Paul?

PAUL: Whereas Madeline swears too much for radio you see, we'd need to beep her. The censorship. Impossible. I tried to get her a job on 'The Real World', but no, 'fuck that', she said.

MADELINE: The repulsive stone-age politics of loud mouth barbaric pig headed males who love the sound of their own voices was also a slight deterrent.

KATE: I may as well have another drink whilst you're making them dear. I've finished my first one.

PAUL: Making. Fixing. Now Spin just to digress momentarily. What exactly are your interests in everything Eastern.

SPIN: Philosophy Sir. Eastern philosophy.

PAUL: Oh?

SPIN: Like Eastern philosophy and how they think and shit.

*SPIN stops. Thinks.*

Right Mad?

MADELINE: It's about letting go of your anger. Releasing futile emotions from the self. Being. Without having to have or want. Trying not to desire things. Is the desired effect. Clarity within the self as paramount –

SPIN: Like with your head space dude. Know what I'm sayin'?

PAUL: Word up bitch.

SPIN: Ha ha! Wicked! Word to the mother totally Mr Cave. Eastern as.

*SPIN can't believe it, he 'hi-fives' PAUL. KATE starts laughing, almost dancing in the hype.*

PAUL: And yes on the topic of 'word up' – you see I would definitely, and Kate I'm sure you'd agree, I would definitely regard myself as a lover of music. Possibly even endow myself an 'aficionado' of everything fine and auditory. For it is my society. But I must be honest with you Spin, I feel hip hop and rap sit outside the term art or music, and in a place of their own more resonant with the sounds of traffic and anarchy.

KATE: We're a bit old-fashioned Spin –

PAUL: I find nothing in their clamour but a catalystic chant to violence and vandalism. Stabbing music. Provoking killings, rape, and graffiti at best.

SPIN: That's frank man. That's totally being frank.

MADELINE: That's not being frank. It's being fucked. What would you know about rap music Paul?

KATE: Squirrel –

MADELINE: Refer to one artist!

PAUL: To my emphatic surprise I can't seem to locate a specific artist – I can, on the other hand, recall some of the oh so elaborate titles these crack head drive by gangster's emblazon themselves with – J-Lo, Ice Box, Niggas Wid Aspertions, Snoop Doggy Snoop –

MADELINE: Rap is the poetry of our people of our time. I wouldn't expect you to understand, let alone attempt to have any kind of insight into what it serves and means. It's electronic and it's brash political and it tells stories –

PAUL: About nailing bitches in the back of your car and shooting brothers in the face. I apologise for my lack of sagacity on the matter but I find it only serves as a fuel for urban warfare –

MADELINE: You never seem to have a problem with warfare in the past Dad, you seem happy to bandy around your Pro confrontation stance every morning on the radio.

PAUL: There must be chaos before calm.

KATE: Oh darling please. Your father and I are heavily involved in several charities and dinners. Um, oh –

PAUL: I find the music just another extension of your 'Because We Can' generation Madeline. Let's put a television in the car, a camera in the phone, a car in the computer, in the phone, in the television, in the computer – 'Because We Can'. Let's download images of Asian teenagers going to the toilet on each other – 'Because We Can'. Let's have filthy aluminium beats dressed up with blasphemous rants of shotgun heroics and call it music – 'Because We Can'.

MADELINE: I'm sorry my generation don't have like a world war or a depression to define us dad but we are an innovative –

45

PAUL: We didn't have a world war dear, we came out of one.

MADELINE: Whatever –

KATE: There was Vietnam. Gorgeous young men.

SPIN: Vietnam was bad ey. So many movies made about that. That was a bad war.

PAUL: I don't think you'll need a world war my dear, you seem to obtain the same results listening to rap music and killing each other yourselves. Or yourselves yourselves.

MADELINE: And what would be the core reason for our fashion of suicide Dad?

PAUL: You tell me Madeline –

MADELINE: There is no such thing as people born bad dad. Just bad parenting.

*Rabbit flutter.*

SPIN: So how was your drive Mrs Cave?

KATE: Oh, lovely thank you Spin.

PAUL: She slept the whole way. A low distorted hum emanating from her left nostril the entire time. I was left with no choice but to plug it up with a ten pound note.

MADELINE: I didn't know you used notes Dad. I thought it was all plastic.

PAUL: I'm becoming traditional of late my dear. I'm becoming very 'real'.

*PAUL directs 'real' to SPIN, who has nodded off.*

I think Spin has spun off to sleep. All that dual showering. Tires the poor boy out Madeline. You must let him bathe alone in future. Purely for his social endurance. Shower in moderation.

*MADELINE moves to SPIN.*

MADELINE: He's not asleep he's – meditating. He's getting – a sense of – to get clarity.

KATE: Grief! That must be a grief thing. Is that a grief thing? Wow. Did they teach him that with the grief? As a grief counselling method?

MADELINE: Ah – yes they did.

KATE: We'll have to look into that for me Paul –

PAUL: Really?

KATE: Grief is so fascinating – isn't it Paul?

PAUL: Is it Kate?

MADELINE: Spin!

*SPIN jolts to attention, knocks the lid off his beer and holds it up in the air.*

SPIN: Here's to family – oil paintings – dual showering – sculptures of motorbikes – permanent drivers – light aeroplanes and –

KATE: Grief.

SPIN: What?

MADELINE: Grief.

SPIN: Word to that –

PAUL: Grief.

*Glasses high in a rough circle. Clink.*

May the devil know you're in heaven half an hour after you're dead.

*They drink.*

*PAUL moves away, leans on the window.*

MADELINE: No dad stay here.

PAUL: Huh?

MADELINE: Come back here.

PAUL: We can vibe down from here.

MADELINE: No, back here. We were almost in a circle.

KATE: Oh, that's gorgeous squirrel.

PAUL: I'm by the window.

MADELINE: I want you back here. In the circle.

PAUL: Are we going to hold hands and sing some early Elton John?

MADELINE: If you like.

KATE: Oh, I do like Elton John.

SPIN: Do you Mrs Cave? I reckon he's damp. Fucken' oily and damp.

KATE: Yes, now I think of it. In those sequined hot pants. He is a spot damp.

MADELINE: Dad!

PAUL: What? I'm perfectly fine here by the window.

MADELINE: Come here. You invented the together. The meet in the middle of the room. You signposted it.

PAUL: I signposted it as a way of beginning. I wanted to share my first drink with you darling – starting with a salute of sorts. Now that is over and done with, and we've all lapsed out of our spiritual trances respectively, we can enjoy the room and our drinks. No need to stay in such a confined spatial relationship.

MADELINE: Just for a minute. I have something to say.

*Rabbit flutter.*

PAUL: So do I. Many things.

KATE: Just come to the circle Paul. For the kiddies.

PAUL: I'm not chanting. Or hugging.

MADELINE: Just come here.

KATE: Paul. It's a good time to, you know!?

SPIN: I'm not going to chant either, if that makes you feel any better Mr Cave. The repetition fucks with me. Mantras and shit.

PAUL: I have nothing against circles Madeline –

MADELINE: Then come here.

PAUL: Circles are fine –

MADELINE: Then come here.

PAUL: It's not the circle that bothers –

MADELINE: Then come here.

KATE: Come on Paul.

SPIN: Come on Paul.

PAUL: Mr Cave to you son.

SPIN: Sir.

MADELINE: Dad.

PAUL: Okay!

*PAUL complies, a circle.*

Circle it is.

KATE: Oh, this is warm isn't it?

SPIN: Full on energy happening Mrs Cave. Totes.

MADELINE: I have something to say.

PAUL: Of course you do. You're a young person. It's all saying and talking. If you're not talking you're texting. If you're not texting –

MADELINE: Shut up Dad –

KATE: Paul, don't blubber. We're in a circle.

PAUL: I know we're in a circle. You don't have to tell me.

SPIN: You know the circle shape is the crux of a lot of Aboriginal paintings Sir? Cos' of the tribes 'n' shit.

PAUL: Spin.

SPIN: Yes, Sir.

PAUL: Spin.

SPIN: You don't have to repeat my name Sir, I'm already scared of you.

PAUL: Oh, you are?

SPIN: Yes, Sir. Everyone is. Whole country.

MADELINE: I have something to say.

KATE: Paul. Madeline has something to say.

PAUL: A quasi scared or an authentic shit scared?

SPIN: Oh, genuine like –

PAUL: Genuine?

MADELINE: Can I but fucking speak!!!???

KATE: Oh.

*Pause.*

MADELINE: I'm dropping out of Law school. I'm going to become – a rap artist.

*Pause.*

PAUL: I think we should change into a square formation.

SPIN: Totally.

KATE: Oh, God I think I may cry.

*Pause.*

MADELINE: I said I'm drop –

PAUL: We heard you.

*Rabbit flutter.*

MADELINE: So that's what I'm doing so you just have to deal with it.

KATE: Is this some kind of funny joke? Spin? Is this how she does a funny joke? Darling? Is this your funny joke?

MADELINE: No, mum. It's fact. I'm dropping out of –

PAUL: I said we heard you.

MADELINE: So react. Come on tough guy. Unearth your dissertation.

PAUL: I honestly don't regard your revolution as worthy of a dissertation Madeline. What do you want me to say? 'Ouch'? 'Bad girl'? Do what you like my dear. It's your life. Be a brave coward.

MADELINE: That doesn't make sense.

PAUL: No Madeline. That's exactly right. It doesn't!

*Rabbit flutter.*

Rap music was ultimately to blame for what happened to Rodney King.

*Rabbit flutter.*

MADELINE: Oh fuck you all!

*MADELINE leaves.*

SPIN: She's totally phat with a p.h. on the mike. Dropping the bomb-arse rhymes. Totes. She really is a dope arse friggin' rapper, man. Mr and Mrs Cave. Poet as.

PAUL: Madeline!

KATE: Don't harass her Paul.

*SPIN beat-boxing and impersonating MADELINE's style.*

SPIN: She's way aggressive but still feminine feline too Mr Cave. Like the blends all tight. And she sits inside the beat all chilled like she was born there. Elbows up by her sides. Boom chi. Boom boo boo chi. Bouncing to the Spin hypnotic death. Kicking like the choo choo train – Insane!

*SPIN completes.*

KATE: Grief can really change you can't it –

*Rabbit flutter.*

PAUL: Baste the rabbit Kate.

KATE: You can't baste a live rabbit.

PAUL: Who says?

SPIN: I was having myself a gander earlier at your produce Mrs Cave and I thought if I got the courage up I would suggest serving the rabbit with a garnish of Burnt cabbage leaves tangled round twice steamed baby carrots with a salt assaulted mess of basted radish stem cucumber skin Spanish onion peel on a bed of French beans and lettuce would be like totally 'fuck off'! Or just a simple jus of lemon rind, cumin with a dash of tamarind. Tamarind is like totally 'the bomb'. Or you could just put it in on its own. Rabbit is quite pungent as its own self. Baked. Casserole. Y'know. Totes.

*Silence.*

I'm going to get another beer.

PAUL: Get me a drink too.

KATE: I'll have one as well.

*SPIN considers the responsibility of getting these drinks, then goes to get them.*

SPIN: Oh, okay.

PAUL: Well you heard the boy Kate, prepare the basting –

KATE: It's alive!

PAUL: Well kill it.

KATE: I'm not killing it.

PAUL: Well just make the baste!

KATE: For a live rabbit?

PAUL: For a live rabbit.

SPIN: Rabbit rocks –

PAUL: Well what are you waiting for?

KATE: I'm scared.

PAUL: Scared of what?

KATE: Scared it will bite me!

*Rabbit flutter.*

SPIN: Is the rabbit still alive?

PAUL: Only way to eat them Spin. Fresh from life. Still thinking. Limbs jiggling in your mouth. Imagination in the marrow.

SPIN: Dude –

PAUL: Mm-mmm!

SPIN: How are you going to kill it?

PAUL: Burn the little bunny in the fireplace. We'll sit around with half empty glasses and watch the little fella burn.

KATE: We don't have any wood Paul.

PAUL: No wood. Hmmm.

SPIN: How would we kill it in a fire without wood?

PAUL: You tell me Spin.

KATE: Let's mull the problem over in our heads.

*They do.*

*MADELINE enters.*

MADELINE: I'm better now that's off my chest. And I'm happy to except all wry jabs of indignation and disappointment. That I'm not to be the girl you wanted me to be. But I'm going to stick by my paradigm shift. As life is not a process of living out other people's fantasies. But it is –

PAUL: Madeline.

MADELINE: No, dad. I won't hear of it. I'm connected to the music. The beat. It's hypnotic.

*SPIN beat boxes. He and MADELINE dance together. Salacious. Hard.*

PAUL: I suppose you're going to tell me you're a drug addict too now?

MADELINE: No, I'm not going to tell you that now.

PAUL: Spin?! Is she? A little mull head? Acid freak? Speed? Hey? Smacky? Crackpot? Coke fiend? On the Charlie? Ey? I'm hip with it. What is she?

SPIN: Au naturale Sir. It's all paw-paw and pilates here dude ey.

PAUL: I'm sorry?

*Dancing stops.*

SPIN: Sir never touched them Sir. Okay, I smoked a little pot at chef school Sir – but that was only to enhance the flavour of the food. Pure as Sir. Eastern as.

*Rabbit flutter.*

PAUL: You know what Spin? Spinner. You and I my boy are going out into the wild thicket of the moonlit jungle to get that empty fire some wood to burn. Then we're going to come back and kill ourselves a rabbit. Are we not?

SPIN: I don't have the proper attire Sir. The beard. The boots. I'm not made for it. I'm the indoors type. Style.

PAUL: Spin? Spin.

SPIN: I'll just be five minutes Sir. Ten. Ten minutes Sir. Five ten. Fifteen. Five.

PAUL: Two minutes.

SPIN: Large.

*SPIN kisses MADELINE and exits.*

MADELINE: You heading out dad. Leaving off.

PAUL: The boy and I are to fetch wood.

MADELINE: Don't feel like staying in here with the women? Too unnerving?

PAUL: We need wood Madeline. If we don't have wood. We have no fire. If we have no fire. We have no killing. If we have no killing –

MADELINE: Yes?

KATE: What was it he said? Radish. Tangled something bed of – tangled bed of – jus? He's such a lovely young man, Mad. Gorgeous facial structure. Lips. The quiff. I love a quiff. And his funny little walk. Like he's half asleep. Oh.

MADELINE: He's the city's hottest hip-hop artist. He introduced the 'n' to drum 'n' bass – that part of the term, to the city. I'm going to be his rapper and dancer. Wearing only light beams. We're doing a national tour. We're called 'Spin Bitch'.

PAUL: 'Spin Bitch'?

KATE: Ha! More!

*KATE moves to the bar.*

MADELINE: You can stop walking around. You can just stand still and stop.

PAUL: I like walking. Gets the brain moving.

MADELINE: Just face me dad.

PAUL: How's the car?

MADELINE: Fuck the car.

PAUL: It's a good car. Why fuck a good car?

KATE: It is a good car.

PAUL: Especially for the city.

KATE: Turns on a ten pence piece.

PAUL: 'What Car' Car of the Year.

KATE: No. Oh, you hear that Mad? Car of the Year!

MADELINE: How does that make you feel Dad? That I'm not going to be a studious little achiever. That I'm going to be butt naked in seedy clubs up and down the country?

KATE: Oh, Mad. Surely you could wear a slip.

MADELINE: Answer me dad. How does that make you feel?

PAUL: I think –

MADELINE: Feel – ?

KATE: Oh, Mad.

PAUL: I think – you'll feel – cold.

MADELINE: Oh, fuck you.

*Rabbit flutter.*

Sliding down the pole. Nude. 'Cos I'm a horny little bitch hardcore. My daddy brought me up to be a spoilt little whore.' Mindless mix of boned up males leering at me. And I'm centre stage, deep throating the mike screaming 'motherfucker' and 'bitch'.

KATE: Very difficult to scream with something in your throat darling.

PAUL: My dear. I'm happy if you're happy.

MADELINE: Ha. Such phoned-in parenting. Get me another martini I'm not numb yet.

PAUL: Kate, martini.

KATE: I can't make martini.

MADELINE: 'How can my daddy know about the real world – when he don't even know, a thing about his little girl.'

PAUL: Just get a curved glass and twist some vodka into it. Then add an olive.

MADELINE: Fuck the olive! Fuck fuck the olive!

PAUL: Or without. Without the olive.

KATE: Paul, tell her –

PAUL: Fix the drink Kate –

MADELINE: What?

KATE: Your father has something to –

PAUL: Curved glass no olive –

MADELINE: What's going on?

PAUL: What's going on?!!! – Ah – Marvin Gaye. 'What's Going On?' There's an artist who knew real suffering. Killed by his father. Though the seeds of his discontent were sown in childhood. Born Marvin Pentz Gaye Junior, Marvin –

KATE: PAUL – now!

PAUL: No, this is relevant! Marvin was the oldest son of a charismatic storefront preacher. On April the first of 1984, in his parents' Los Angeles home, Marvin had a go at his old man for verbally abusing his mother. His father responded by shooting his son to death – using a gun that Marvin himself had given him four months earlier – thus putting to rest a bitter, life-long Oedipal struggle.

KATE: How is that relevant Paul? Come on. Sharpen up.

PAUL: Well you'd like to kill me wouldn't you Madeline?

*Rabbit flutter.*

MADELINE: Being your daughter is hard.

PAUL: I apologise for success.

MADELINE: Success? There's a concept. Try walking round campus – Paul Cave's daughter. Feel the inferred hatred rising up off the library lawn –

PAUL: Oh how I adore seated activism –

MADELINE: Dad, I'm hated. Everybody hates me. Even the lecturers.

KATE: Well you do put together some very odd outfits –

PAUL: Education is not meant to be a party my dear –

MADELINE: Dad they hate me because they know who I am. They know I'm the daughter of the man who cajoles this country into the kingdom of fear and political droopiness in which it lives.

PAUL: Let me digest these modern terms for a second –

MADELINE: Are we firing up? Are we bickering? Are we on air?

KATE: No please –

PAUL: I'll win.

MADELINE: You always win.

PAUL: I'm a winner.

MADELINE: Dad.

PAUL: Darling.

MADELINE: Stand still.

PAUL: In a circle not in a circle?

MADELINE: Dad.

PAUL: Okay what? What? Fucking what!?

MADELINE: I hate you.

*Rabbit flutter.*

I hate you.

PAUL: Giving in and dropping out –

59

MADELINE: Don't flatter yourself –

KATE: Enough please –

MADELINE: I do. I hate you –

PAUL: Of course you do. It's easier that way –

KATE: No, she doesn't. Do you?

MADELINE: In my dreams. There is a basement. The walls are made from the flesh of rotting bats. There is no floor. Just black air. And you. In the corner. With a microphone. And a dwarf. Eating your face.

PAUL: Oh, we don't write them like we used to.

MADELINE: Stay with me dad I haven't finished yet. Don't run off to your gabble.

PAUL: I'm here. With my dwarf.

MADELINE: Dad. I hate you. I have to tell you that. I need you to know that. And the more you buy me. And the more you preach your palaver. The more you push me to hate. You push it into me. Like mercury. I can feel it in my bones. You and the you I Hate.

KATE: Where did you learn to talk like this?

MADELINE: How does that make you feel? That your only child hates you?

*PAUL downs a drink. Another.*

KATE: Where do we keep the board games – ?

MADELINE: Shut up Mum! (*Same time.*)

PAUL: Shut up Kate!

KATE: Spin!

*Rabbit flutter.*

PAUL: I like your boyfriend.

MADELINE: Yeah. So do I. He's an honest person. He loves me for who I am. He sees my thoughts because he wants them. He's beautiful.

PAUL: I never did anything to hurt you. I hardly drink anymore. Never hit you.

MADELINE: You never hit me because you were never in arm's reach. You sit on mike barking on about 'the real world' –

KATE: Oh, must we? Look outside at the poinsettia.

MADELINE: There's one photo. I have in my drawer. All stained and bent. Of you. And me. In the sandpit. I was six in a Barbie tutu. And you have your hand in my hair. Your other hand holding a book. That's pretty much it. The only photo where you're showing affection. And you're not even looking at me. You're reading your own autobiography.

PAUL: Hmm. I'm sorry my dear, I have very little time for victims. You know that half of the living world has never made or received a phone call?! I think you're doing okay –

MADELINE: See me. In your holiday house. Your daughter. And know that I hate you.

*Pause.*

PAUL: I introduced you to Frank Sinatra – remember – when you were a kid – we used to sing together – 'the way you wear your hat – the way you dance till – '

MADELINE: Frank Sinatra is dead!

*PAUL swipes the food off the bench. KATE goes to clean it up.*

KATE: Look what you've done –

PAUL: Leave it!!

KATE: You happy now Madeline Cave? You've upset things.

*Rabbit flutter.*

How are we going to kill this rabbit everyone!?

MADELINE: Get dad to look at it. It'll die of emptiness. I need another drink. Make me a drink daddy. Get me things daddy. Buy me things daddy. Fix me things daddy. I'm going to throw my body all over the insides of drug houses up and down this country and everyone will know that I am Paul Cave's daughter. The infamous Paul Cave. The voice of 'The Real World'. And look at his daughter. What a shameless slut. What a deplorable whore. I'm going to fuck your career daddy. Because that's the only thing you have for me to get at.

*PAUL drinks two drinks.*

KATE: Where's all this coming from? I thought we were going to have a nice weekend in the hills. Look at twilight. The purples. Look at all the purples.

MADELINE: I have to change who I am – because of you.

PAUL: And who are you Madeline?

MADELINE: No one you know!

PAUL: Madeline.

MADELINE: Don't say my name. Don't say it. You don't know it. Don't love it. Don't say it. Ever again.

*Rabbit flutter.*

PAUL: Okay. And what would you like to conclude with?

KATE: I think it's over already isn't it – ?

MADELINE: I'm just not into it. Sitting here all weekend like a happy family. Putting on a show. Tomorrow I could find my death and die, and I'm not going to die with a blocked soul. I'm getting it out. Eastern.

62

PAUL: Okay. You've got a shit dad. What's your point?

MADELINE: My point is. Don't fuck with my life.

PAUL: Fuck with your life how?

MADELINE: You know how.

PAUL: No I don't. Tell me. Tell me how on earth could I possibly fuck with your life now!? Go on tell me! Tell me!!! Fucking tell me?!!!!!

*They face each other with so much need.*

Let me off Mad. Let me go.

MADELINE: I don't know what I'm saying –

PAUL: Let your old man go. Mad –

MADELINE: Go where? Dad go where?

*PAUL takes her by the thumbs.*

PAUL: I –

*SPIN enters dressed for wood. Belt dangling from his arm.*

SPIN: Let's go get wood and shit.

*Rabbit flutter. Silence.*

PAUL: I'll get the axes.

*PAUL leaves.*

SPIN: I'm going out with Paul to get wood and shit.

*Silence.*

Did someone die in here?

KATE: You have a belt around your arm Spin.

SPIN: Oh. Yeah. I have a –

KATE: Concentrated blood pressure? You need to –

SPIN: Concentrate my blood into –

KATE: Sections of your arm. I wanted to be a nurse once believe it or not.

*KATE releases the belt.*

Haemoglobin anaemia. Fatigue.

SPIN: Yeah. I'm constantly fatigued by my globin.

MADELINE: Fatigue is also symptom of heroin abuse – I read that somewhere.

*KATE scoffs a laugh.*

KATE: Spin do you think you could manage to kill the rabbit when you come back?

SPIN: Word to that Mrs Cave. Do you have a shot gun? Uzi?

KATE: Ah. No.

SPIN: Then I'll beat the bitch with my own knuckles, word.

KATE: Yes! Your very own hands! Ha!

*PAUL enters with two axes.*

PAUL: Axes!

SPIN: Fuck ey. Gotta go be a man. Ah, let's talk rabbit murder later on Mrs Cave. I'm off and into it. Love you baby.

KATE: (*Soft.*) Baby –

*SPIN kisses MADELINE, takes an axe from a brazen PAUL. The two men stand together facing the two women. Stillness. After a while the men grunt a little and leave.*

*KATE smells her wine.*

Oh. Oh, how I love pinot noir. Smells like vomit.

*KATE gulps.*

Tastes like the forest.

*Rabbit flutter.*

God knows why we couldn't just have venison or something already dead.

MADELINE: Take him out of the box.

KATE: You do it. You're street-wise.

MADELINE: Fine I'll tip it out the window. Solved.

*MADELINE attempts to pick up the box, KATE stops her.*

KATE: No. Stand back. Your father wants dead rabbit basted then that's what he gets.

MADELINE: Whatever dad wants.

KATE: You should have respect for your father. He does a lot for you.

MADELINE: He does it with money, mum. Cars. Phones. Rent. Spin says: The more plastic parenting you receive the more you lack in such things as independence, self worth and – other things. Dad has denied me my right to learn how to live in the real world.

KATE: Well darling why don't you give back the money, hand over the car, return the phone, move out of the apartment?! He's not forcing them on you.

MADELINE: I've adjusted. I'm conditioned now. I'd be lost without my things.

KATE: And that's our fault?!

*Rabbit flutter.*

(*Focussed.*) I'm going to drop it from the roof.

MADELINE: That won't kill it.

KATE: Well, what will? If he wants killing then there must be killing.

MADELINE: Stop serving him.

KATE: Oh!? I'll be bored out of my mind with too much money.

MADELINE: Ah, have you ever heard of the concept of having your own life?

KATE: Yes Madeline I have. But I'm not selfish like you people. Go on living in small flats across the Metropolitan and not breeding. Drinking red drinks and meeting to discuss your 'head space'. I live in the real world where women savour life. Not see therapists about its dips and complexities.

MADELINE: Whatever.

KATE: That's exactly right. That's all you people ever say. Whatever. Whatever. Oh, whatever!

MADELINE: Whatever.

*KATE takes the bottle, steps up to rage.*

KATE: I carried you in my womb Madeline! I cleaned your bony arse for years. I lost the shape of my breasts and believe you me young lady I had a pair of breasts that could knock a man off his bar stool from a hundred feet.

MADELINE: Mum you need a therapist.

KATE: Maybe I could go to yours darling. The one that costs your father an arm and a leg. Get a two for one mother daughter deal. Me? Therapy? Ha! You really are quite unreal!

*KATE tips the bottle into her throat.*

*Rabbit flutter.*

*KATE grins.*

Maddy –

MADELINE: What? What the fuck?

KATE: There's more to it.

MADELINE: What? More to what? To life? No shit.

KATE: To this. Weekend. There's more.

MADELINE: Well why don't you tell me what it is then?

KATE: This is going to sound very big but it's really quite natural.

MADELINE: Big how? Mum big how?

KATE: Big as it gets darling. Big as it gets.

MADELINE: Okay. Fuck mum. I don't. Know how ready I am. For anything.

KATE: Your father. Has.

*MADELINE starts to breathe fast.*

*Rabbit flutters constant through –*

MADELINE: Mum. No. Okay. No. Come on. No.

KATE: Hmm. Your father. For a while now.

MADELINE: What? No. Mum. Say it. What?

KATE: Your father has.

MADELINE: No. Okay. What?

KATE: Your father –

MADELINE: No. Okay.

KATE: Your father has –

MADELINE: No. Okay.

KATE: Your father has –

MADELINE: No, please.

KATE: Ah. Your father.

MADELINE: No. Mum. No –

KATE: Your father has –

MADELINE: No. No.

KATE: Your –

MADELINE: No. Okay.

KATE: Your father has –

MADELINE: No. Okay.

KATE: Your –

MADELINE: What!?

KATE: Your father has been dying!

*Rabbit stops flutter.*

For a while. Such a while that he is no longer dying but almost dead. Three weeks. A month. A week. A night. An hour. He won't make Christmas. So don't get him anything.

*Rabbit flutter. MADELINE's breathing hastens. Rabbit flutter. Breathing hastens. Rabbit flutters. Breathing. Rabbit. Breathing. Rabbit. MADELINE screams at the top of her lungs and stops. Rabbit.*

Shut up you silly little Rabbit!!!

*Black.*

*Light.*

*Woods. Night is trying to fall.*

*SPIN has a big bottle of beer.*

SPIN: Ah. Squish.

PAUL: Feel the earth my boy.

SPIN: I'm feeling it. In my socks. Up my leg.

PAUL: We could walk forever. As men.

SPIN: I swear there was wood back there Mr Cave.

PAUL: Paul. Call me Paul.

SPIN: Paul. I swear there was wood back there Sir. Back there closer to the house.

PAUL: Towards the moon. Into the light. Savage white light.

SPIN: Totally. I swear there was wood back there Paul.

PAUL: Son. There's wood everywhere in the woods.

SPIN: Yeah. Is there a particular kind I should be looking out for?

PAUL: I should have stuck to squash. I was a fabulous squash player. Puritanical. Clannish white man dominating small black ball. Thwap! In my shorts. Hovering over black lines. And now look at me. Mouth on mike jawbone drop the argy-bargy. Action is a real man's business. Action and whacking. That's the 'real world'. I should've lived in the real world.

SPIN: Sir, the reeds are getting taller.

*SPIN slaps his face madly.*

I have web on my face!

*Black.*

*Light.*

*House.*

*MADELINE is being calmed by her mother.*

*DRIVER enters.*

MADELINE: Aah! What the fuck is that?!

KATE: Oh, hello Driver. Everything okay in the car?

DRIVER: Yes, Ma'am. The car is fine.

KATE: Oh, good. Oh, good.

MADELINE: Who is that? Mum –

DRIVER: I was wondering Mrs Cave. If you could tell me the whereabouts of Mr Cave.

KATE: Mr Cave is getting wood Driver. Perhaps you should assist him.

DRIVER: Yes, Ma'am.

*DRIVER goes to leave.*

KATE: Oh, have you killed rabbits before Driver?

DRIVER: No, Ma'am.

MADELINE: Who is this man?

DRIVER: I am Driver.

KATE: He's Driver.

MADELINE: You're Driver.

DRIVER: Yes. Yes. I am Driver.

MADELINE: That's your name.

KATE: That's what he does.

MADELINE: Is Driver your name or is driver what you do?

KATE: That's irrelevant darling, he's Driver.

MADELINE: What's your name?

KATE: I don't think we really need to know do we?

DRIVER: My name? My name is –

KATE: That'll do Driver. What's your purpose?

DRIVER: Find Mr Cave.

KATE: He's gathering wood Driver. What can I do for you? Would you like to use the toilet?

DRIVER: No, Ma'am. I wanted to expand on my original request for a brief leave of absence.

KATE: Hmm. Paul did say –

DRIVER: I've been on the phone to my wife see.

KATE: The phone we pay for?

DRIVER: Yes. Separate sim but yes. The doctors are not sure if my son will make it through the night.

MADELINE: Your son?

KATE: Driver has a one-year-old son, yes.

DRIVER: Yes, my son. He's. He's ill.

MADELINE: Well go see him. God. Go. Bye.

DRIVER: Thank you Ma'am.

KATE: No no no. I'm afraid Paul must give you the permission for leave Driver.

MADELINE: It's his fucking son! Just go.

DRIVER: Thank you Madeline.

KATE: Just toddle on down to the woods and confront him there. Thank you Driver.

MADELINE: Fuck 'em Driver. Just go.

DRIVER: Thank you again young Miss. I really do appreciate your insight into the core of the dilemma. But, apparently there is such a thing as definition.

KATE: That's right. Definition. Exactly. What is defined. Exactly. Yes. That's right. I say yes. No. Definition!

DRIVER: So, I am to find Mr Cave. Do it the right way. I apologise for the interruption.

*DRIVER takes a moment. DRIVER leaves.*

*Black.*

*Light.*

*Woods.*

*Men are far from home.*

PAUL: We're getting closer. The sky is opening up. The gates.

SPIN: Sir, there's no gate. And the sky man, like, Sir. I have to stop and have some beer I'm in a pant.

*They stop. SPIN drinks beer.*

Would you like some Sir? Paul?

PAUL: I'm going to take my clothes off.

SPIN: Sir, no.

PAUL: How does that make you feel?

SPIN: Sir, I've lost the capacity to feel. It's more of a visual concern.

PAUL: I've always been confronting. Let us shed the wrappers of humanity. Throw organs to the wind.

SPIN: Sir, I don't wanna see your gear. It'll – I'm sure it'll change my relationship with your daughter. I'll look at her and see – I dunno. I feel vulnerable to that now.

*PAUL naked.*

PAUL: Ah, all off.

SPIN: Oh fuck man, it's all there.

PAUL: I am so here.

SPIN: Man, I go with your daughter.

PAUL: My daughter. My prostate once led my daughter to her life. My prostate. Now corrupts my fate. There's irony. On a rare evening in the back seat of my helicopter, this fluid, this alkaline fluid, burrowed out of it's prostatic ducts, slid down my member, picking up my daughter, enhancing her in volume, comfort, and transport, and moved her safely into the free-range eggs of my wife.

SPIN: Sir, what is this man? I need more beer.

PAUL: My prostate. The place, the sack, the clutch, from which my fate now rack and ruin.

SPIN: Shit dude.

PAUL: You know what I want to know about?

*SPIN picks up PAUL's pants.*

SPIN: You really should put these back on. If not just the pants man.

PAUL: I want to talk about your dead parents.

SPIN: Oh, dude. Nudity and death man.

PAUL: Let's talk death with the night.

SPIN: My head's cracking as it is Sir.

PAUL: Tell me about being left.

SPIN: Dude.

PAUL: Dude.

SPIN: Mr Cave.

PAUL: Paul.

SPIN: Sir.

PAUL: May I call you son?

SPIN: Oh, man.

PAUL: I like the sound of it. Son. May I call you son?

SPIN: Sir, this is not some weird sex thing – ?

PAUL: Everything is sex my boy. Why do we polish our
     floorboards? Buy red cars? Apply hair product?

SPIN: I do very little with my hair Sir.

*PAUL holds his arms out.*

PAUL: See me Spin? See this man?

SPIN: Yeah. I do Sir.

PAUL: This man is made of cancer. He should be dead.

*Pause.*

SPIN: That's not that good.

*Pause.*

How long have you known this?

PAUL: Eighteen months ago they found it. I thought oh, it's
     only prostate. Now. Now it's all of me. Good night.

*PAUL crumbles down.*

SPIN: Why haven't you told Madeline?

*PAUL looks to SPIN, smiles tender and weak.*

*Black.*

*Light.*

*House.*

*KATE pours from many bottles into a glass.*

MADELINE: This can't happen.

KATE: Well it is.

MADELINE: What?

KATE: I said well it is.

MADELINE: Well it can't.

KATE: Well it fucking well is.

MADELINE: Well it fucking well can't.

KATE: Well fuck.

MADELINE: It can't.

KATE: Can.

MADELINE: It won't.

KATE: Will.

MADELINE: It doesn't. Not to me. Stop this. Shut it off at the gate. No. Not happening.

KATE: Oh, I'm afraid it is squirrel.

*MADELINE's breathing takes her over.*

MADELINE: No. No. No. No. No.

KATE: Yep. Yep. Yep. Yep. Yep.

*MADELINE takes a deep breath.*

MADELINE: What about herbs? Natural herbs? Yes! Natural herbs! Do we have any parsley! Mum! Surely there's a natural way to – the way you wear your –

*Rabbit flutter.*

KATE: Will you please but fucking die!

*Black.*

*Light.*

*Woods.*

PAUL: I didn't want to interrupt her studies. She's one year from finishing. And she gets –

SPIN: Anxious –

PAUL: The attacks. I thought best not to burden her.

SPIN: You have to burden her Paul.

PAUL: I have to be here. With you son. Under the circus tent sky. Making my way to the other side.

SPIN: Hoo – this feels pretty warped ey. I'd prefer to be in the house. With the sculpture. And the rabbit!

PAUL: Ah! Rabbit! Mrs Rabbit always told her little rabbits, 'Don't you go wandering into Mr McGregor's garden. Or he'll put you in his pie. That's what he did to your father.'

SPIN: Have a serious drink. Y'know. Sit down with Mad. Have it out. Totes.

PAUL: But Peter, who was very naughty, ran straight to Mr McGregor's garden, and squeezed under the gate!

SPIN: What gate? Dude fuck!?

*Black.*

*Light.*

*House.*

*MADELINE looks out the window for her father.*

*KATE smiles at her own thoughts.*

*A dark well of silence.*

*Black.*

*Light.*

*Woods. Story telling.*

PAUL: And Pete. The little rascal rabbit – Peter Rabbit started hoeing into the cabbages and beans. Devouring the radishes and carrots. Devouring all the veg. But round the end of a cucumber frame, whom should he meet but Mr McGregor! Waving his rake and screaming 'Stop Thief!' Peter ran for his life. But he got caught in the gooseberry net. Losing his jacket. The blue jacket with brass buttons. Quite new. Peter gave himself up for lost, and shed big tears. But his sobs were overheard by some friendly sparrows, who flew to him in great excitement, and implored him to exert himself. Exert himself. Mr McGregor. Who had put Peter's dad in a pie, came up with a big sieve, intending to pop poor Peter with it. But Peter wriggled away. Full of tears and fears. Leaving his blue jacket. Quite new. In the netting behind him.

*PAUL shakes.*

He was scared that little Peter Rabbit. Scared for his life.

SPIN: Shit man. And then what happened to the little dude.

PAUL: And then Mr Mac hung up his jacket to scare away the blackbirds. Hung it up like a scarecrow. Effectively.

SPIN: And Pete didn't die? Not like his dad ey. Who ended up in the pie. Please no – please don't let him die.

PAUL: No. He ran past Mr McGregor and through the gate.

SPIN: Mr McGregor didn't pop him or nothing?

PAUL: No. He didn't seem to care. He let him pass. Under the gate.

SPIN: Phew!

PAUL: Peter made it home. Mrs Rabbit made him tea. It was the second jacket he'd lost in a fortnight. See. So.

SPIN: There was.

PAUL: An understanding.

SPIN: Between Mr Mac – ?!

PAUL: And the rabbit. A sort of –

*The men look at each other.*

*Black.*

*Light.*

*House.*

*MADELINE rocks back and forth, crying.*

*KATE chops food messily.*

KATE: Stop crying.

*MADELINE rocks and cries.*

I said stop crying.

*MADELINE rocks and cries.*

I said stop crying!

MADELINE: Why?! Why fuck would I stop crying!?

*MADELINE rocks and cries harder.*

KATE: I wasn't aware we mourned for those we hate.

*MADELINE rocks to a stop.*

I'm just quoting.

*MADELINE rocks again.*

MADELINE: Mum?

KATE: Yes squirrel.

MADELINE: I wish it was you.

*MADELINE gets up and exits to the hall.*

*Black.*

*Light.*

*Woods.*

SPIN: It was a hobby. The light plane thing. We were on a
vineyard. They went up on Sundays. Mum dad. All
locked up in a long love. They'd been sippin' the new
vintage all arvo. Y'know. We were on a vineyard. That
was our trade. To make the grapes up and turn them into
God's bottle. I was washing the skins with the snake
hose. We'd just picked see. Exciting time of year. For the
makers. Day breakers. I had my young head all tilted up
watching the makers that made me – make their way
through the burnt orange mosaic sky. The perfect hour
they framed it. Floating all lost. They'd been sipping all
arvo. The pulp. Tasting the new batch. Wondered what
they said as they fell. Flat. Into the crop. Dad's body
expressed itself like a Pollock on the window. Mum's
head on top of the hill. Like the hill was her body. And
her head still in life on it. Lips still quivering. Mouthing
'Spin. Spin.' The burnt orange sky burning my heart out.
My dropped hose flailing pain. And I knew I didn't feel

that good. And I knew I didn't feel that bad. I just knew
I'd be okay from now on. Cos' – I had an excuse.

*Long silence.*

*Black.*

*Light.*

*House.*

*KATE in a drunken dream world.*

KATE: Kate Cave. 'Bra's'. No. Kate Cave. 'Sheer black
frocks'. No. No. Kate Cave. 'Intimate Apparel'. Yes! Yes!
Yes! 'Kate Cave Intimate Apparel For The Posh And
Filthy!' Hoo-hoo!

*KATE raises a glass to herself.*

*Black.*

*Light.*

*Woods.*

PAUL: My brother died on a bench outside a church with a
needle in his eyeball. A 'Choose Your Own Adventure'
novel sliding down between his knees. There's an
emblem.

SPIN: What drug Sir?

PAUL: Heroin. What else I ask you?

SPIN: I'm on heroin Sir.

*Pause.*

Right now Sir.

*Pause.*

To be honest. Man to man. Like. Yeah. I'm totally caned
on the gear. Right now. Stoned. Whacked. Clubbed.

Cunted. On the hammer. The horse. Which Sir. I bought. With your money ey. And have been. Every day. For ages.

*Silence.*

*They stare into each other. PAUL takes his hand. SPIN takes them both in his other. PAUL puts his other on top. Joined.*

*A creeping noise. SPIN breaks off.*

Sir – shoosh. Do you hear something?

*They listen. Louder creeping.*

Someone's coming. Can you hear that?

PAUL: I hear progress.

SPIN: Oh frig man.

*Creeping louder and louder.*

PAUL: It must be the devil. I've always wanted to meet him.

SPIN: Dude. Listen to the steps. It's like a total squad of yetis are coming down the hill.

PAUL: Ominous. Come to me, oh blackest hour.

SPIN: Dude. If it is the devil. Shouldn't you put some clothing back on?

PAUL: Take me through the gaps in the black air and into the forever.

SPIN: Dude, stop with the mortality shit. There's totally a bear coming towards us.

PAUL: I had a cross-court backhand the best you'd ever see. Squash was my game. Squash!

SPIN: Where did we leave the axes? We need them axes!

PAUL: Come to me, oh beast of blackness. Show me the end. Know that I am naked Mr Beast. As you unload your wrath. Know the extent of my nakedness.

SPIN: And know this Mr Beast. I hardly know this man. I'm merely courting his only child. That's a thin thread. We're by no means members of the same anything. We may have divulged a bit. But believe me please I beg you! We're from polar universes. Paul let's go man, let's run. I'm no coward Mr Cave. I just love your daughter.

PAUL: We all do son. Some of us are lucky enough to voice it.

*SPIN takes PAUL's shirt, ties it round his head.*

SPIN: Good then. See you back there. God bless. AAAAaaaaaaararrrrgghghghghghgh!!!!!!!!!!!!!

*SPIN takes off, screaming with his bottle in the air.*

*PAUL hangs his jacket on a stick like a scarecrow.*

*PAUL takes a couple of tree branches and fixes them to his head like headphones, talks into a branch.*

PAUL: Hello. Paul Cave. The Real World. How can I help you?

*Pause. Louder creeping.*

Turn me off. Take out the DAT tapes. Peel off the spines. On Air. Flashing. Red to cherry dead. To deep red black. Delay. And off. Take me off. The air. Too much talk-back. Always. Talking back. Welcome back. This is the time in the following places. I'm going to arc up about this. I'll be taking calls from the bewildered, lonely, and acerbic. I am the voice of truth, beauty, and endorsement. I launch myself into the air. Turn it off. Pike. Spin. Spiral down into the microphone. Forever. On Air. Off Air. I'm taking calls from the dead. In the real world.

*DRIVER enters.*

DRIVER: Ah, Sir.

PAUL: Yes, I've been expecting you.

DRIVER: Sir. Mr Cave.

PAUL: Yes, Fate.

DRIVER: Here. Put my coat on.

PAUL: If that's what it takes.

*DRIVER puts the coat on PAUL.*

DRIVER: Sir, I've been on the phone to the hospital. And I think I may need to go as they – they are not sure if my boy will make it through.

PAUL: Is this purgatory? Is that what this is?

DRIVER: So, because I am a 'permanent driver'. I feel I may have to resign and go see my sick kid. So as not to meddle with definition. That's the road I'm heading down anyway. Of latest thought.

PAUL: Have you ever killed a rabbit, Fate?

DRIVER: No, Sir. Your wife asked me –

PAUL: Neither have I. Let's go.

DRIVER: Yes, Sir. Where Sir?

PAUL: To save your kid. Where there's death there's life. Go Fate. Go. To the boy.

DRIVER: Oh, Sir. You're a remarkable man.

PAUL: Let us go! Time is small.

DRIVER: But Sir. One thing.

PAUL: Yes?

DRIVER: If we go now –

PAUL: Yes Fate?

DRIVER: Will I still be Driver?

*Black.*

*Light.*

*House.*

*MADELINE enters, dressed down and for the cold.*

MADELINE: Mum, you're smiling.

KATE: No, I'm not.

MADELINE: Yes you are.

KATE: No, I'm not.

MADELINE: Look at you!

KATE: Yes Madeline. Okay yes. You got me. Fucking yes. Fuck me I'm smiling. Yes! I've spent the last twenty-seven years in a public stoning. Taking the force of your fathers blows in the face of high society. I've held my breath, held my mouth, held him up, held it all. And now I'm free from under it. I'm peeling back the rock. Much beauty groweth from dead soil. Or something.

*Pause. MADELINE heads for the door.*

Where are you going squirrel?

MADELINE: I'm going to find my father.

KATE: Darling stay in here you'll catch a chill.

MADELINE: A chill?!!! A chill?!!!

*SPIN enters shuddering with need.*

SPIN: Where's my shit?!

MADELINE: Baby!

*MADELINE rushes to him. He slips through.*

SPIN: Get me my shit baby. I need a hit like I'll never love again.

MADELINE: Baby –

KATE: Baby –

SPIN: It is the strangest night. Your dad, man. He's lost the handle. He's all nude and wild man. Coming onto the moon. Freaking totally. And the yetis man. Where's my fucking gear?

MADELINE: That's my father's shirt –

KATE: What gear?

SPIN: My fucking gear Mrs Cave. My smack. My shit. Whatever.

KATE: It's for grief – ?

SPIN: Yeah. Whatever. My grief killer. Yeah.

KATE: Will it kill the rabbit?

SPIN: What?

MADELINE: Why do you have my father's shirt!?

KATE: Will your killer kill the rabbit?

MADELINE: What happened to him?!

SPIN: Shit man your olds are totes whacked. Frig I need some shit in me babe. Get me my shit babes!

MADELINE: Where's my father?

SPIN: Babes my gear.

MADELINE: Tell me where my father is – !

SPIN: Look, fuck it. I'll tell you everything. Just get me a whack and I'll totes tell ya everything. Everything. Promise. Baby fuck. Respect the neeeeeeeeeed!!!

*MADELINE exits, swift as hell.*

What the fuck are you looking at?

*Pause. They look at each other.*

Oh I don't give a shit who you are this whole thing is loopy as. Totally loopy. Beyatch.

KATE: Where is Paul?

SPIN: He's out there with the yeti man.

KATE: The what?

SPIN: Madeline! Hurry up! The yeti woman. The yeti.

KATE: Did you see Driver?

SPIN: Frig I'm sweating internally.

KATE: Did you see Driver?

SPIN: Driver?

KATE: A big man called Driver?

SPIN: The big hard looking guy in a suit?

KATE: Yes.

SPIN: Why? Should I?

KATE: I sent him down to see you.

SPIN: You sent – ?

KATE: Driver.

SPIN: Driver the big guy.

KATE: Yes.

SPIN: Hmm. That puts a spin on things.

*MADELINE enters throwing the pack. SPIN unfolds it. Preps.*

Oh baby. God bless the earth that moves beneath you.

MADELINE: Whatever. Where is my father?

SPIN: Hoo. 'Tis the strangest night homes. Motho – fohka!

MADELINE: Spin?

SPIN: Yes baby.

*MADELINE slaps him hard.*

Fuck! What was that for?

MADELINE: Where is my father? Tell me now.

SPIN: He's out there with the night baby. Get us one of them Belgian beers?

MADELINE: Tell me where the fuck he is!

SPIN: Chill baby.

*SPIN cooks the spoon.*

MADELINE: Tell me now!

SPIN: He's out there babes. Somewhere between the real world and the next one. I got this habit see. Of leaving parents in the woods. When they're still kickin'. Ooh, it's hard being me. I tell ya'. It's hard being a man who lets things slide. So –

*SPIN shoots up.*

I cooked up enough for two here baby. You in?

*SPIN pulls it out of his arm. Offers it up.*

*MADELINE leaves.*

*SPIN is frozen. KATE stares at SPIN's arm. Goes to him. Takes the syringe. Walks back over to the rabbit box. Opens it. Rabbit flutters. KATE plunges the syringe into the rabbit. Sighs relief. SPIN spirals.*

*Black.*

*Light.*

*Woods. PAUL can't see.*

PAUL: Hello Paul Cave Real World attention Staff. We're here for the child. Is the child dead? We're here for the child. Round up, round up, we're requesting a child. Sorry? Yes Paul Cave from The Real World that's me. No, no pants tonight. It's just a choice not to – choices! That's right. We're here to put life back into the kid. We're here to bring the kid back to life. Driver's kid. We're here for the kid am I making myself clear?

DRIVER: Sir! The car is this way Sir. This way. With me.

*PAUL fends DRIVER off.*

PAUL: For 'the boy'. He's one tonight and he needs a few things. Money. A car. And some parents. Bit of time from the parents. Get by with a little help. From the parents.

DRIVER: Sir, please! Come on. This way. Sir!

*PAUL evades him. Falls. Stands.*

PAUL: Where are the three wise men? What were there names Driver?

DRIVER: Balthazar and – can't recall Sir.

PAUL: Ain't that just the way it is. We remember what they brought but not what their names were. We're here for the kid the boy the son. Driver's son. My driver's son. Don't touch me.

DRIVER: Sir! Please Sir. Don't let me down.

PAUL: Ey. Don't surround me. Can't catch me. I'm sorry coats of white. What's Going On?!

DRIVER: Sir, please Sir this is life and death –

PAUL: Ow! I'm here to get a kid from the jaws of death. That's right. The clutch. Me. And the kid. In the clutch. We're all kids. In the clutch. In the beginning. And in the end. We are children. Helpless. Lost. Futile. Naked. Real.

DRIVER: Please Sir we need to get out of the woods!

*Driver grabs PAUL harshly. Looks into him.*

Oh, no.

*Black.*

*Light.*

*Woods.*

*MADELINE raps furious.*

MADELINE: Ladies and gentleman of this theatre of tear drops may we please address the inevitable. In this impenetrable – forest of bass and treble – check the levels – cos Daddy I never felt so terrible. Sick to my heart – I must impart – this revelation – that puts a permanent stain on my generation. The questions I'm so afraid I hold the answer – in the truth of night daddy I believe I am your cancer. For my adolescence – I offer up my penance – but ten thousand Hail Mary's wont eradicate the memory – of the whinging cataclysmic concert of narcissism – we broke you down with the relentless sound – of our 'poor me' voices – cos we got choices – 'don't mess with my head space daddy I'm afraid I'll crisis'. In this fateful prison I threw you – from here on in without you – I corrupted you – from head to toe – with my ungrateful 'do what I want to do' – spoilt brat know it all fuck you all. Tall poppy – I'm going shopping for some jeans that are more distressed than me. Like a little red riding hood – I sailed though my childhood – messing with the big bad wolf. Not only did I bite off the hand that feeds me – I took a chunk out of the stomach of the man who's seedling – I am – disgraced – off my face – my soul is dead – fuck you Edith Piaf I'm going to have regrets. Cos' there is no consolation – in this night sky no constellation – to soften my damnation – if only we could begin again – I would serve you learn from you be your friend. But it's too late now cos' you're at your end – death is the question I have the answer – I'm sorry daddy I think I am your cancer. So on behalf of my peers I'd like to file this statement – that we are the poison in this curious ailment. Now I know why cancer effects every family – cos their kids make em so sick to the stomach they can't handle it. Daddy forever from you my heart is torn – somebody find me a pair of the devil's horns!

*MADELINE stops rapping. Looks around for PAUL.*

Daddy. I've come for you. Sing to me.

*Black.*

*Light.*

*House. SPIN is out to it.*

*KATE is madly chopping and ripping open vegetables. She wears a slip under an apron and it is evident she has skinned the rabbit from the blood all over her.*

*SPIN comes to half life in a nightmare.*

SPIN: Muuuuuuuuuuuuummmmmmmmmmmmm!!!!!!!!!!

*SPIN falls back again. Gone. Black.*

*Black.*

*Light.*

*Woods.*

*PAUL looks for MADELINE.*

PAUL: Our romance won't end on a sorrowful note.
Though by tomorrow you're gone. The song is ended
but as the song writer wrote. The melody lingers on.
They may take you from me, I'll miss your fond caress.
But though they take you from me, I still possess – The
way you wear your hat.

*MADELINE looks for PAUL.*

MADELINE: The way you sip your tea.

PAUL: The memory of all that.

MADELINE: Oh no. They can't take you away from me.

PAUL: I know I was a shit Dad.

MADELINE: You never looked for me.

PAUL: And, I'm aware of that.

MADELINE: Come on Dad, why didn't you tell me?

PAUL: We may never never meet again.

MADELINE: On the bumpy road of life.

PAUL: You know I'll always always love that little girl –

DRIVER: The angel of your eye.

PAUL: The way you looked at three.

MADELINE: And now you leave my life.

PAUL: No –

MADELINE: Dad, you're a cunt for never telling me.

PAUL: No, no.

MADELINE: You're a cunt for never telling me.

*Pause.*

Daddy?!?!?!?!?!?!?!

*PAUL goes to speak. Can't. His voice is gone forever.*

*Black.*

*Light.*

*House.*

*KATE swirls the baste. She is even slinkier.*

*SPIN wakes to her sprinkling baste on him.*

KATE: Morning dear.

SPIN: Mum?

KATE: Basting happy.

SPIN: Hoo. There's a woman who makes you feel not too far away. Wassup Mrs C?

KATE: You're up Spin. Time for you to inherit a little bit of manliness.

SPIN: I'm sorry.

KATE: Don't be. Come to the women Spin.

*KATE pours baste over the rabbit. Stuffs produce into its rear.*

SPIN: The what?

KATE: You know we have more houses than the average person has t-shirts. More boats. Helicopters. Shares. We have a house for filing. Time for Spin to step up to bat!

SPIN: (*Sad.*) Shit. (*Shock.*) Fuck. (*Joy.*) Bitch!

*SPIN spins. KATE stuffs, bastes, and giggles. Getting even slinkier.*

You know what this is?

KATE: A twisted bed of –

SPIN: This is like some kind of reverse karma parent vibe fiasco! Like I'm getting it all from losing it all.

KATE: That's exactly what it is Spinner. It's karma with a capital K! Come to the women Spin. We'll be family.

SPIN: We'll be family?

KATE: We'll be family.

*KATE steps to him.*

SPIN: We'll be family.

*KATE moves his head into her chest. Strokes it. He smiles.*

KATE: That's it. That's it. That's my little Peter Rabbit.

*Black.*

*Light.*

*Woods.*

*DRIVER is in tears on his phone.*

DRIVER: Please. Someone put me near my son's face. Just put it near his face. On his skin. Please? Just rest the phone on his cheek. I want to kiss him goodnight. Oh, my boy. Goodbye my boy. I. I love you.

*DRIVER kisses the phone.*

*Black.*

*Light.*

*Woods.*

*MADELINE shudders in shock at the scarecrow like thing in her path. She then realises it is her father's coat. Takes it off the branch. Smells it. Puts it on. Picks up his trousers.*

*Black.*

*Light.*

*House.*

*SPIN sets the table. KATE instructs.*

SPIN: Madeline next to Paul here.

KATE: Yes! Paul there Paul there.

SPIN: And me right across from you.

KATE: Oh, we can clock each other in good humour.

*They laugh.*

SPIN: It's going to be just lovely.

KATE: Work from the outside in –

SPIN: Always.

KATE: Wine glasses –

SPIN: On the right. Right?

KATE: Right.

SPIN: Aw, my baby's gonna love this spread.

KATE: Ironic rabbit!

SPIN: Ironic rabbit!

KATE: Ironic rabbit!

SPIN: Family facing each other with their faces. Every thing in its place.

KATE: Everything in its right place.

SPIN: Everything in its place.

KATE: Everything is going to be alright.

SPIN: Everything. Absolutely everything has turned out alright. It's all alright.

KATE: That's right. You're right.

SPIN: Everything.

KATE: Everything.

*SPIN finishes setting.*

SPIN: Everything. Ah.

*SPIN faces KATE. KATE glares a grin.*

What?

*Black.*

*Light.*

*Woods.*

*PAUL spins in the night, lost.*

*MADELINE enters. They face each other. Silence.*

*They approach each other. PAUL runs his fingers through her hair. Touches her face. She touches his.*

*MADELINE hands him his trousers. Puts them on.*

*PAUL hums the first line of 'Can't Take That Away from Me'. MADELINE hums it back. They hum together. Slow dancing. Duet humming. Dressing.*

*Black.*

*Light.*

*House.*

*KATE claps. SPIN raps.*

SPIN: Comes a moment in a young mans life – where ya'
gotta step up and stare the beast in the eye. There's a day
in your life – where you meet with your dream. Take the
bull by the horns – put your balls on the guillotine!

KATE: A pow wow wow yippo yo yippy yay.

SPIN: A pow wow wow that day was today. I stepped out
into the night with the man Mr Cave. He handed me an
axe – I gripped the handle raised the blade. I stood my
ground – Stepped up – Stared him right in the eye.
Thinkin' bitch: I'm the daddy now – I ain't gonna lie. I
got you Paul Cave – I see the cracks. There's no myth
here – Just death and tax. I'm in the real world with The
Real World himself. My fears fall away with my main
man's health. We lanced through the jungle comin' to
grips with shit. Truth and lying' – death and dying – two
dudes kickin it. But then the sky froze up – Paul got hit
with the fears. Like a crumbling mess – tumbling tears.
The Gods told me I was needed. So I took his hand and I
squeezed it. I felt the weight – in his puff cold sighs. The
shudder in his nerves – cracks in his eyes. I threw all my
grief into his hand until it stopped. I felt it stop – All the
shudder – All the fear. And I released him forever –
Forever from here. A free man who's ass I saved – Yeah
that's right bitch I freed Paul Cave! I can be this Kate. I
can see this Kate. I can nail this Kate. It's a
mutherfucken date. If I was Shakespeare – Then this
would be my sonnet. But instead this is the block and
I'm the new kid on it!!!

*Rap stops.*

I just need seventy-two hours in a small room with a shit
load of Zoloft – Prozac – Rohypnol – Morphine –
Methadone – Orange Juice and we can do this!

KATE: My man. All class.

SPIN: The world's an oyster in a shot glass.

KATE: We'll kill rabbits.

SPIN: Millions of them.

KATE: You and me.

SPIN: You and me.

> *SPIN spins to her. A moment. KATE kisses him. SPIN breaks free.*

Don't challenge me Kate my parents are dead!

> *Pause.*

KATE: You're the king of the castle.

> *Pause.*

SPIN: And you're the dirty rascal – ?

> *KATE nods. Pause.*

> *SPIN lopes over.*

SPIN: Baby?

> *They kiss. Her mostly. Then he joins. Evil passion.*

> *MADELINE and PAUL enter carrying axes. They watch. Then, simultaneously drop their axes. KATE and SPIN separate.*

KATE: Enchanté! You're to sit here Paul. And Madeline just across from your father there. And I and Spin over here and here yes! Oh!

> *PAUL and MADELINE sit on the ground.*

> *KATE brings over the rabbit.*

> *SPIN pours wine.*

SPIN: Ironic rabbit with a grief and devil sauce. Pinot noir woir? Yes. I think so. For you. For you. And – for you. Not for me. I'm taking it easy. Too much to think about. Hoo. Well no fuss. Get into it Paul. Mad!?

*SPIN offers it to MADELINE, KATE stops him.*

KATE: Maddy is a vegan!

SPIN: Of course. Well, I'm a little full myself.

KATE: So am I.

*SPIN places the rabbit on PAUL's plate.*

SPIN: So, looks like it's all yours Mr Cave. Dive right in. Your favourite. Recently dead rabbit.

KATE: Let's say Grace.

SPIN: Grace. Ha!

*KATE and SPIN suppress giggling.*

*A circle.*

KATE: A prayer.

SPIN: A prayer –

*They all look up.*

KATE: Dear God –

*Nothing.*

Dear family.

SPIN: Dear family. Yes. That's better.

KATE: May we live in the real world forever.

SPIN: Forever.

KATE: Forever.

SPIN: Amen.

KATE: Amen.

*Pause.*

SPIN: To dead grapes and dead rabbits!

KATE: Grapes and rabbits.

SPIN: Dead.

KATE: No regrets?

SPIN: No regrets.

*All glasses raised.*

PAUL: (*So soft – almost only mouthed.*) Amen.

*They drink. KATE and SPIN suppress giggling.*

*PAUL cuts into the rabbit, takes it to his mouth.*

*Suddenly – DRIVER enters. Dishevelled. He has a phone in his hand. A voice rattles within it. He goes to PAUL, who is inches from eating.*

DRIVER: Mr Cave. Ah. My wife's on the phone. Mr Cave. She wants to talk to you Sir. On your phone. Talk to you on the phone you gave me. Separate sim but. It's your phone Sir. By definition.

*PAUL goes to eat, DRIVER grabs his wrist. DRIVER holds the phone.*

Sir? She wants some advice. From the man who knows about the real world. Sir? She wants to know.

*DRIVER takes the phone to his own ear.*

Hang on baby I'm just putting him on.

*DRIVER puts the phone to PAUL's ear.*

Sir! My wife wants some advice from Paul Cave. Paul
Cave from The Real World. She wants to know what to
do. Sir. Sir. Paul.

*DRIVER kneels down next to PAUL.*

Sir. With a dead son. In The Real World. Look at me!
Look at me you cunt! What do you do with a dead son?
Sir.

*DRIVER takes PAUL's shoulders in his hands. DRIVER cries.*

Sir. My wife. She's a big fan. Of your show. She wants
some talkback with you. Needs! She needs to know Mr
Cave. What to do – with a dead son. In The Real World?

*DRIVER releases PAUL's wrist. PAUL eats. Chewing.*

Sir. My name's Paul too.

*DRIVER places his phone down. A voice rattles within it.*

*SPIN gets up, fists clenched.*

SPIN: One more second and I would've –

KATE: I know baby.

*SPIN sits.*

*PAUL eats more rabbit. Chews. Slower. Slower. Slower.
Overdose. PAUL dies.*

*MADELINE picks up the phone.*

MADELINE: Hello. Madeline Cave. The Real World. How
can I help you?

*Black.*